# container gardening in Hawai'i

# container gardening in Hawai'i

## How to Grow Paradise in a Pot

Janice Crowl

Mutual Publishing

Library of Congress Cataloging-in-Publication Data

Crowl, Janice.
Container gardening in Hawaii : how to grow paradise in a pot / Janice Crowl.
p. cm.
Includes bibliographical references and index.
ISBN 1-56647-836-7 (softcover : alk. paper)
1. Container gardening--Hawaii. I. Title.
SB418.C76 2007
635.9'8609969--dc22
2007019118

ISBN-10: 1-56647-836-7
ISBN-13: 978-1-56647-836-6

Design by Nancy Watanabe

First Printing, August 2007
1 2 3 4 5 6 7 8 9

Mutual Publishing, LLC
1215 Center Street, Suite 210
Honolulu, Hawaii 96816
Ph: (808) 732-1709
Fax: (808) 734-4094
email: info@mutualpublishing.com
www.mutualpublishing.com

Printed in Korea

# Table of Contents

# Acknowledgments

Contained within this book are the contributions of many generous spirits.

Mahalo to horticulturalist and sustainable landscaping consultant Heidi Bornhorst; University of Hawai'i at Mānoa Cooperative Extension Service county agents Andrew Kawabata and Debbie Ward (retired), and extension specialist Dr. Scot Nelson, who reviewed the manuscript in its entirety and gave many invaluable, insightful suggestions; UH researcher Dr. Bernard Kratky and United States Department of Agriculture scientist Dr. Francis Zee, who reviewed the sections that pertain to their research; faculty and staff of the UHM College of Tropical Agriculture and Human Resources Cooperative Extension Service at the Komohana Complex in Hilo who always responded to my frequent requests for information; Rick Barboza (native Hawaiian plants), Piper Selden (worm composting), Susan Ruskin and Peter Berg (noninvasive bamboo), who provided assistance in their areas of expertise; numerous garden retailers and plant nursery owners and staff who allowed me to "talk story" and to photograph in their establishments; my fellow gardeners who allowed me to photograph their fantastic gardens and experience their wisdom and camaraderie; and antique collectors and local artists who are involved with pottery and art for the garden, including Ira Ono, founder/director of Volcano Garden Arts, where many photos were taken.

My children, Laurel and Drew Planas, and friends let me pull them into service as models, go-fers, and "composters of pilikia" while they pushed me to the finish line. On them I dump heaps of love and gratitude and double rainbows forever.

To all on the path, my aloha and many, many thanks. May your gardens always fill you with joy, wherever your paradise grows.

Janice Crowl
Hilo, Hawai'i

# 1 Container Gardening is Growing in Hawai‘i

Energy seems to emanate from this "meditator" with tall narrow-bladed New Zealand flax (*Phormium* hybrid) rising behind it. Purple and violet blossoms, as well as burgundy and green foliage, frame the focal point with full layers.

Isolated in the vast Pacific Ocean, Hawai‘i is a tiny island oasis, a garden contained and embraced by the sea. People all over the world think of Hawai‘i as a lush tropical paradise where exotic plants grow throughout the year. However, land available for human activity has always been limited in Hawai‘i, and modern development has dramatically changed the landscape. Land once alive with native vegetation, taro fields, and sugar/pineapple plantations now supports high-rise and suburban communities. Hawai‘i is continually changing, and our Island attitudes and lifestyles are evolving in response. These days an aspiring green thumb might not have much land in which to plant a garden, much less have the time to maintain a full-scale one.

(right): Before, a drab, nondescript walkway to a front door practically begs for some TLC.

(below): After, refreshing pinks and whites brighten up an inviting pathway. Sprucing up the pavers and adding container plantings liven up the entryway.

Still, wherever we live in Hawaiʻi, the weather is warm and the natural beauty of the Islands beckons to our primal selves. We are never too far from being surrounded by cool greenery and the sweet scent of blossoms wafting on gentle breezes. Even when we might not even be aware of their presence, plants thrive and persist in releasing life-giving oxygen, which soothes and revives us. It does not matter if you live in an apartment, in a newly built dream house atop black pāhoehoe and red cinder, or in a classic kamaʻāina home with stately palms and luxuriant lawns. A bit of vibrant living color on a patio or lanai is a visual reminder of the paradise you live in, the landscape that comes to mind with the phrase "Lucky you live Hawaiʻi." Indeed, Hawaiʻi nō ka ʻoi.

Container gardens are growing in popularity in the Islands because they are quick, convenient, and provide instant gratification. You can invest as much or as little as you want in a container, whatever suits your fancy: a set of shiny new copper boxes, a one-of-a-kind antique ceramic planter, a modest plastic pot, or even a recycled rubber tire. Container gardening makes it easy to grow in ways and in places you might not have thought possible. If you want an Island-style garden without too much fuss and hard work, container gardening provides many solutions.

## Good Reasons for Containers

### Grow a garden where there is limited or no soil.

If you have a garden outside a first floor condominium or apartment, you can increase the planting area with containers. Even if you are on the second story or above you can still enjoy a living touch of Hawaiʻi, personally created by you with container plantings. Barren areas go from blah to bountiful with colors, textures, shapes, and fragrances.

**Overcome problems with poor soil.**
Planting in containers helps you to avoid common problems associated with planting in Hawai'i garden soil, such as root knot nematode or bacterial wilt and other soil-borne diseases.

**Save money.**
With enough light you can grow your own mini-farm of fresh herbs, fruits, and vegetables just steps from the kitchen. Cut down a little on your food bill and know exactly how fresh your food is and how it was grown. Nothing beats a homegrown tomato!

Grow tender Mānoa lettuce (*Lactuca sativa* 'Manoa') in a window box with only 4 to 6 hours of filtered sun. Store leftover seeds in an airtight container in the refrigerator to keep them fresh for the next planting.

Native Hawaiian palapalai fern (*Microlepia strigosa*) is an important plant among hula dancers, who use it to adorn themselves and hula altars. With enough humidity, it looks great outdoors on a partially shaded lanai or under bright, filtered light indoors.

**Save time.**
You don't have to wait for seeds to grow to see flowers outside your window when you purchase starter plants in bloom. When one plant is spent, just slip in another one.

**Maximize space.**
Containers make a small garden look bigger yet are easier to maintain.

**Move with ease.**
Container plantings are like furniture. If you are bored with the same tired garden plan, you can rearrange containers to create new landscaping layouts. You can easily move plantings around when necessary if they are in lightweight containers or on casters. If growing conditions change, you can relocate your plants to protect them or to take

advantage of the environment. For instance, if there is too much rain you can move plants to shelter, or if conditions are too hot and dry you can move plants to shade. If you move to another home, you might even be able to pack up your garden and go!

**Blend the natural beauty of Hawai'i with your home.**

You can use container plantings to frame a view or to screen an undesirable one. Create a transition from indoor to outdoor living with container plantings that complement the design of your home.

Container plantings visually extend the indoor living space of this patio in Mountain View, Hawai'i, to the forest outdoors.

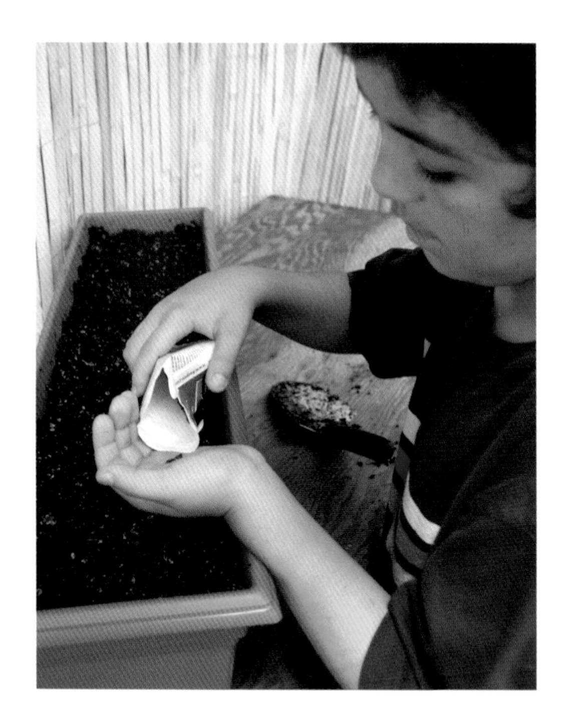

Container gardens are fun-filled educational projects for kids. Let them make a list of what they want to grow. Watering and caring for container plantings teaches them responsibility and gives them a sense of accomplishment. Growing edibles teaches them about nutrition and how their food is grown.

### Garden with ʻohana.

Container gardens are accessible and fun for children and seniors. You can eliminate stooping and heavy lifting by placing everything at a convenient height. Persons with physical challenges often find that gardening in containers minimizes frustration and gives them great pleasure and satisfaction.

### Control damage to plants, ensure safety.

Hanging containers or placing them off the ground limits damage to plants from slugs, snails, and ants, reducing the need for chemical pesticides. If you are growing plants that have poisonous or prickly parts, you can safeguard small children from danger. Plants can be placed out of reach of cats, dogs, chickens, goats, and other uninvited grazers. Tip: Catnip is easy to grow and can be a delightful treat for your pet. Grown in a hanging basket, it can be plucked at any time but kept out of kitty's reach.

### Keep rampant growth in check.

Some plants, such as bamboo and bougainvillea, can aggressively grow into other parts of your garden and soon you have more yard work than you want. Although you might not want these plants in the ground, you can still enjoy them by restricting their growth to containers. However, if a plant is

This tropical pitcher plant, *Nepenthes*, is possibly the easiest carnivorous plant to grow. This one grows best hanging in a humid, sheltered area with bright, filtered sunlight and away from the wind. Hapless flies and other insects are attracted to the fragrant fluid in the "pitcher," become trapped inside and then drown, becoming nutrition for the plant. The pitcher actually grows at the end of the leaf and has a digestive gland.

regarded as a highly invasive pest in your area, the best idea is to not plant it at all. According to the state of Hawaiʻi Department of Land and Natural Resources and the Department of Forestry and Wildlife, approximately 70 percent of all documented invasive species in Hawaiʻi started out as seemingly harmless ornamentals. Although you might try to be diligent about keeping a plant from escaping the container, wind, birds, or other visitors to your garden can scatter seeds or other plant parts that can take root. Gardeners have a profound impact on Hawaiʻi's ecosystems. Let's act responsibly to protect and conserve Hawaiʻi's native habitats for future generations.

(left): Bougainvillea is beloved by Hawaiʻi gardeners because it is easy to grow and available in a generous palette of brilliant colors. Some varieties can grow extremely fast under the right conditions and can quickly take up space. Planting in containers keeps it confined, and regular pruning keeps it tidy.

(right): "Found" items from nature sing of the beauty of the Islands. Driftwood and lauaʻe fern (*Microsorum scolopendria*) play a counterpoint with coleus (*Coleus x hybridus*) and portulaca (*Portulaca grandiflora*) in a terra-cotta clay pot.

# 2 The Basics

## CONTAINERS

There are many types of containers available in retail garden shops. Each type has characteristics that will affect the success of your plantings. Keep these qualities in mind when choosing a container. Think about the needs of the plants you will grow and where you will keep them. Imagine how the container will look in the location you will place it. Visualize the scale, style, and colors of the surrounding area. The best strategy is to take a photo of the location and bring it with you when you go shopping.

Enjoy exploring the options! You might discover you like the look of clay but want something that won't break as easily. A terra-cotta colored plastic pot is an inexpensive substitute. If you think large concrete or stone planters are lovely to look at but too

Unglazed clay pots are available in a wide range of shapes and sizes. They are porous and therefore "breathe," meaning oxygen and water move more freely in and out of the pot, so there is less chance of root rot.

A single, large pot can be a strong decorative element all on its own. Choose a design that will complement the form of the plant, and vice versa. Also consider the surrounding decor. This fantastic ocean-themed mosaic pot would look right at home on a beachfront lanai.

heavy and expensive, try some impressive imitators, such as the sturdy ones made out of a combination of synthetic and natural materials.

Here are the most common types of containers sold by Hawai'i retailers.

## Clay

**Unglazed clay** pots of terra-cotta are what most people think of when asked to describe a flowerpot. When left unglazed, clay is "breathable," or porous, allowing plant roots to receive the air they need for healthy growth. The porosity of unglazed clay allows salts from fertilizers to move to the outside of the pot, so there is less buildup of chemicals that can be toxic to the plant. These salts, and some that are naturally present in the clay itself, form a white patina on the outside surface.

Plants that prefer to dry between watering do well in clay pots. However, if you live on the leeward side in an area prone to hot, dry, windy conditions, an unglazed clay pot can allow moisture to evaporate too quickly. In hot weather, containers of unglazed clay might require watering at least twice a day, and extremely dry conditions could require watering several times a day—too much work, and not water-efficient. Large pots retain moisture better than small ones, so under dry conditions try using pots at least 12 inches in diameter. You can also try planting in a plastic pot first and then slip it into a larger clay pot. Use cinder as mulch,

Use a sealer on the inside of clay pots before painting the outside with acrylic paint. That way the paint won't peel off once the clay becomes wet from watering. You can add seashells, beach glass, or tiles using concrete grout or a hot glue gun.

or blue rock gravel for extra weight in windy areas. Fill in the spaces between the inner pot and outer pot with cinder to hide the plastic pot. Your plants benefit from the water-retaining properties of plastic, and you still get to enjoy the beauty of bona fide clay.

Saucers of unglazed clay catch runoff but because they are porous they can also allow a small amount of moisture to seep through and damage moisture-sensitive surfaces. A container that sits in the hot sun on a concrete patio might be helped by unglazed clay pot "feet." Pot feet provide better exposure to air and allow pots to stay cooler. Pot feet sometimes come in whimsical shapes. Frog-shaped ones don't seem to ward off coqui frogs, but they do make visitors smile.

Clay has a natural presence that complements nearly every setting, casual or

(left): Brush on yogurt or buttermilk with some ground-up moss to accelerate the weathering process.

(below): High gloss, smooth glazes have a formal air. Pots with rough textures and matte glazes from China and Vietnam are popular for their earthy, rustic look.

formal. Its versatility makes it easy to match it with containers made of other materials, too. Other advantages of unglazed clay are that it is relatively inexpensive and easy to paint, or decorate with tile, shells, or beach glass. If you like an aged look, leave an unglazed clay pot in a wet, shady corner of the yard for several weeks to let it acquire a coat of moss and algae. Mosses are acid-loving plants, and you can speed up the moss-growing process by brushing on buttermilk or yogurt, which are naturally acidic. Add in a little ground-up moss to give it a headstart.

(right): Put unglazed clay pots in a shady, moist place for a month or so to grow moss on them.

To clean algae and moss from pots, scrub with a paste of baking soda and water. If you want to sterilize used clay pots to make them free from pathogens that can cause disease, soak them in a 10 percent bleach solution (1 part bleach, 9 parts water) for 10 minutes. Wear old clothes and protect your hands with rubber gloves. Rinse the pots thoroughly.

(below): These concrete pots, sold in a Big Island garden shop, were handmade by an 81-year-old plantation retiree who had been making them for over 30 years.

**Glazed clay** containers are more expensive. These come in an array of glazes and patterns to coordinate with Chinese, Japanese, Balinese, and other Asian-inspired themes. Glazed clay is nonporous, and a pot without drainage holes and sealed on the inside is perfect for a water garden. Or you can use it as a cachepot to dress up a plant you want to keep in its plain plastic nursery pot and prevent water runoff indoors or outdoors.

Large clay containers are heavy and provide more stability. When planting a

large pot, first place it in its desired location and then fill it with potting mix. Otherwise, it will be too heavy to move when you are done. A platform with casters, sometimes called a plant trolley or caddy, is convenient for moving heavy containers. Clay is fragile, so use extra care when relocating these containers. *Another note of caution:* Large clay containers might be too heavy for your balcony or rooftop. Check with your building manager for weight load restrictions if you live above the ground floor.

## Concrete

Concrete containers are hefty and stable, semiporous but strong. Concrete darkens with age and sometimes will grow moss. These containers are popular with bonsai enthusiasts. Sleek and stylish terazzo planters are also made of concrete. These are finished with mortar and bits of marble, and then given a high polish. If you like the appearance of concrete but want a lighter, cheaper substitute, roll up your sleeves and get creative with **hypertufa**. (See Chapter 3 for instructions on how to make a hypertufa container.)

These sophisticated, modern terrazzo pots from Vietnam are made of concrete that was finished with bits of marble and polished smooth.

## Wood

Wooden containers are semiporous and naturally insulating. They stay cool in hot weather and hold moisture fairly well. In dry climates, containers of redwood, cedar, and teak are rot resistant. However, when weather is warm and humid year-round, wood breaks down faster, which is

Wooden containers can be store-bought, or you can build your own design.

Galvanized steel tubs and buckets can be used for ornamentals in interior or exterior settings. Shiny metal containers highlight plants with silvery leaves or light gray-green succulents and cacti.

Metal hayrack planters have coir liners that can hold pots or potting mix.

something to keep in mind if you live on the wet, windward sides of the Islands. Hawai'i gardeners occasionally have to contend with termites, too. Wine or whiskey wooden half-barrels are large enough for small trees or companion plantings of vegetables. Drill at least four or five 1-inch holes for adequate drainage. Use bricks to allow air to circulate under the barrel. It's a good idea to raise the barrel off a concrete patio that gets hot. Bricks can also keep wooden containers above the soggy ground, which might hasten decay and attract termites. Some shops sell rigid plastic liners and kits that turn a wooden half-barrel into an instant no-fuss water garden.

## Metal

Upscale metal containers of copper, iron, and lead are uncommon in Hawai'i. These containers are available through garden suppliers via mail order and online retailers, but shipping costs are high. If you do obtain one of these containers it will last a lifetime, taking on a fine patina. On the other end of the price range are inexpensive galvanized steel containers. They can work in a modern, industrial interiorscape or in a theme recalling Hawai'i's plantation days. Look for shiny new pails and washtubs in hardware and farm supply stores. The zinc finish on galvanized steel will dull and rust eventually, but some folks think that's part of its appeal. Most people use metal containers as a decorative shell for a plant grown in a clay or plastic pot. Punch drainage holes in the bottoms of galvanized steel containers with a hammer and nail if you want to plant directly in them, but know that it is possible for zinc to leach into the potting mix. Plant ornamentals, or use a plastic liner for edibles to avoid consuming heavy metals.

Metal wire baskets lined with sphagnum moss or coir (coconut fiber) let roots stay cool and aerated. Such baskets dry out quickly and require frequent watering. These are

better kept in indirect sun and away from too much wind. Metal hayrack planters with coir liners can be used outdoors as window boxes or indoors as wall accents.

## Plastic and Foam

Functionality and affordability make up for the humble aesthetic of plastic. Plastic containers are nonporous and retain water well, which is helpful in situations where other types of containers dry out too quickly. Very thirsty plants such as vegetables are easier to keep moist in plastic containers. Some plastic containers are self-watering with an interior reservoir for added convenience. Plastic containers are lightweight, which is good if you have weight restrictions for your balcony or rooftop and want to use large pots. However, small plastic pots can get knocked over easily in high traffic areas or by strong gusts of wind. Heavy-duty plastic is virtually indestructible. Cheap pots get weathered quickly and eventually crack.

(above): They may look like stone, but fiberglass, resin, and stone composites are a fraction of the weight.

(left): Plastic is a versatile, economical choice. Plastic hanging pots are lightweight and retain moisture well. Remove a saucer attached to the bottom if you want to increase drainage.

Plastic pots can heat up in the hot sun, especially dark-colored ones. If your plants will be on a sun-drenched concrete patio, try white or light colored plastic pots to reflect light and heat and keep plant roots cooler.

Foam is another inexpensive material that is sometimes made to look like stone, but foam containers of low quality are damaged easily and can look bad quickly. However, good quality foam containers are lightweight and are useful in large sizes.

### Fiberglass, Resin/Stone Composites

Containers of fiberglass or resin and stone composites are tough, lightweight alternatives that mimic the appearance of stone and concrete. Unlike their genuine cousins, these fabulous fakes are nonporous. Many of them are cleverly crafted to look distressed—no waiting for that coveted antique look. There is a wide variety of classic urn shapes, faux stone textures, and colors available. Fiberglass is the most expensive synthetic material for containers, and it will last for many years. Synthetic containers usually have a plug you can remove for drainage if you are planting directly into the container, or you can leave it in if you plan to keep a plant in its nursery pot.

### Woven Baskets

Bamboo, rattan, coconut, lau hala, and other natural fibers tell Pacific and Asian stories. You're sure to find a basket that fits your budget and style, from affordable to artisan. Put a plastic saucer in the bottom of the basket to catch water that drains from the pot. Remove the water whenever it collects. Most plants don't thrive if their roots remain underwater. If you want to plant directly into a basket, line it with coir or sphagnum moss and then fill it with potting mix.

## DRAINAGE

Good drainage is the key to growing healthy plants in containers. Being a container gardener is a bit like being a zookeeper. That is, you have to meet the needs of anything that is being kept, and some specimens adapt better to confinement than others. Plants

Baskets are excellent "coverups" for plants in plastic pots, and they have casual warmth that enhances a tropical atmosphere.

## Characteristics of Containers

| CONTAINER TYPE | POROSITY | WEIGHT | COST | STRENGTH |
|---|---|---|---|---|
| Unglazed clay | Porous | Medium to Heavy | Low to Moderate | Fragile |
| Glazed clay | Nonporous | Medium to Heavy | Moderate to High | Fragile |
| Concrete | Semiporous | Heavy | Moderate to High | Durable |
| Wood | Semiporous | Medium to Heavy | Moderate | Somewhat durable |
| Galvanized steel | Nonporous | Light to Medium | Low to Moderate | Somewhat durable |
| Copper, Iron, Lead | Nonporous | Heavy | High | Very durable |
| Plastic & Foam | Nonporous | Light | Low to Moderate | Somewhat durable |
| Fiberglass | Nonporous | Light | High | Very durable |
| Resin/Stone Composite | Nonporous | Light | Moderate to High | Very durable |
| Woven Basket | Highly porous | Light | Low to Moderate | Fragile |

can't escape from unhealthy conditions that can develop within the container. For the majority of plants, a container that retains too much water will create an environment that drowns the roots and eventually kills the plant. Make sure there are adequate drainage holes in the bottom of the container before planting.

Always remove standing water from a saucer or cachepot soon after watering to prevent the chance of root rot and to eliminate a breeding ground for mosquitoes. If a potted plant is too large and heavy to lift from its saucer or cachepot, use a kitchen meat baster (the kind that looks like a giant eyedropper) to extract accumulated water. To make sure plant roots get enough exposure to air, place the pot atop something that will elevate it out of water that may collect. Use a pair of evenly spaced wooden chopsticks, a smaller inverted pot or saucer, or a brick (or a similar object) as spacers.

Drainage holes generally should be about ½-inch diameter, but large containers such as wooden barrels need 1-inch holes. To drill in clay, use a masonry drill bit.

To improve drainage many Hawai'i gardeners incorporate 1 part volcanic cinder to 2 parts potting mix, or even 1 part cinder to 1 part potting mix, depending on the type of plant and where it will be kept.

## POTTING MIX

Potting soil, or potting mix, isn't actually soil but is a soilless combination of ingredients, or media, formulated especially for growing plants in containers. You might be tempted to use regular garden soil straight from your yard to fill a pot—it's free, right? You might be successful using garden soil, but there are some caveats. Soil is limited in Hawai'i, and the quality of the soil varies widely. Most garden soil doesn't drain well in containers. Even if you add amendments to improve the drainage of garden soil, ready-made potting mix is a lot easier to manage because it has been processed to eliminate weed seeds, soil organisms, and insects that can cause problems. You can try sterilizing your home garden soil by heating it in your kitchen oven but it's likely to end up a smelly day at home that was better spent at the beach. Sterilizing also kills off beneficial fungi and other helpful organisms. Auwē! But if you are determined to use your own garden soil, the University of Hawai'i Cooperative Extension Service recommends that you have your garden soil tested before you mix it with amendments so that you understand what it needs and eliminate the guesswork. See the suggested recipe in this chapter for making your own potting mix from garden soil.

Potting mix provides physical support for the plant, water retention, aeration, and drainage. Garden shops usually carry an assortment of commercially made potting mixes to suit a variety of planting needs. Potting mixes differ in composition and cost per unit, and it pays to read the labels and compare the contents to understand what you're getting for your money. Most potting mixes are primarily a blend of peat and perlite but can also include composted bark, coir (coconut fiber), vermiculite, sand, cinder, clay, and other materials.

Fresh potting mix is a good investment for healthy container-growing. Although it might seem economical to reuse old media, there are hazards; a buildup of fertilizer salts can lead to poor plant health, and diseases in old media can be transmitted to the new plants.

## Potting Mix Ingredients

These are the most common ingredients included in commercial potting mix.

**Peat.** Peat is decomposed vegetation including various aquatic plants and peat moss, which is sphagnum moss usually imported from Canada. Peat has excellent water-retaining capabilities but it is difficult to moisten when dry, so potting mixes usually contain a wetting agent. There has been concern about the environmental impact of harvesting peat bogs, which are important habitats for wildlife and protect the earth from global warming. Whereas Canadian sphagnum peat seems plentiful and only about 1 percent of the total is harvested each year, peat resources in the United States are limited and are composed mainly of reedsedges from sensitive wetlands. Coir, or coconut fiber, is a renewable substitute for peat.

**Perlite.** It may look a little like puffed white rice but perlite is actually a type of volcanic glass that expands when heated at extremely high temperature. Perlite is sterile, doesn't decompose, and improves aeration and drainage. Coarse perlite lasts longer. If you want to add perlite to a potting mix, wet the perlite beforehand to reduce your chance of breathing in dust.

**Vermiculite.** When the volcanic clay called mica is superheated it expands and produces a spongy, "wormy" material called vermiculite that breaks apart easily. Vermiculite holds water and improves drainage. It retains more water than perlite does and it is sterile, making it an excellent material in which to root cuttings. For this purpose it is used alone or mixed with perlite. In long-term plantings, vermiculite eventually collapses, which can lead to poor aeration. Avoid breathing the dust of

(clockwise from upper left): vermiculite, Canadian sphagnum moss, commercial compost, perlite.

Organic fertilizers such as kelp meal, bone meal, rock phosphate, and greensand provide slow-release nutrition. Dolomite is a source of lime to adjust the pH of the potting mix, plus it adds calcium and magnesium.

vermiculite, as the dust can irritate your lungs.

**Bark, Coir.** Coir, shredded bark, and composted bark provide some aeration and water retention. Finer composted bark is similar to peat in its ability to retain water.

**Clay.** Clay doesn't decompose and it has a high capacity for retaining water, so it is used as only part of a potting mix.

**Sand.** An appropriate amount of coral sand can improve aeration, add weight, and contribute a liming agent that affects the pH of the potting mix.

**Cinder.** Some Mainland-made commercial potting mixes list cinder as an ingredient. Cinder has excellent water retention and aeration properties. Many Island gardeners like to add Hawai'i's volcanic cinder to their potting mix for better drainage. Cinder makes a pot heavier and less easy to knock over. On the Big Island, cinder is readily available and relatively inexpensive, making it a favorite of local gardeners. Commercial growers of orchids and tropical rhododendrons, or vireyas, use cinder because of the excellent drainage required by these plants.

Should you use black cinder or red cinder? More research is needed on these as growing media to determine actual differences and advantages, other than aesthetics, between the different kinds of cinder. Cinder is obtained from several different locations on the Big Island, and the characteristics of the cinder can vary greatly. If you prefer, you can rinse cinder before using it to remove dust that can cause compaction and poor aeration, and to leach out soluble calcium, magnesium, and sodium that might affect pH. A popular mix for Hawai'i container gardens is a well-draining blend of 1 part cinder to 2 parts potting mix.

(clockwise from upper left): black cinder, red cinder, coconut coir chips, decorative wood chips ("bark").

## Types of Potting Mixes

Most potting mixes right off the shelf already contain fertilizers. Some mixes have little added nutrients, others have the kind of fertilizer that is used up quickly, and some more expensive brands also contain slow-release fertilizer. If you are using large amounts of potting mix, it is often cheaper to add your own slow-release fertilizer. Most potting mixes have a slightly acidic pH of 5.0 to 6.5, which allows the plant to take up nutrients. Lime is sometimes listed on the label of a potting mix because it is used to adjust the pH of the potting mix.

In addition to general-purpose types, there are a variety of commercially made potting mixes designed to meet specific planting needs. For instance, cactus mix is a light, fast-draining blend with more perlite added. Organic potting mixes are typically fortified with products such as compost and organic fertilizers that provide good structure and break down over time, slowly releasing nutrients. These potting mixes can be expensive but they may be worth the added cost if you want to grow only a few organic edibles in containers. Plants grown in organic potting mix also benefit from a regular schedule of organic liquid fertilizer applications to maintain healthy growth. See Chapter 6 for more about growing organically.

I spoke with many veteran gardeners who, like seasoned chefs, had created their own custom recipes after years of experimentation. They learned to adjust their mixes for the type of plant and the conditions of the growing environment. If you like experimenting, presented here is a basic do-it-yourself recipe for an organic soilless potting mix from the Appropriate Technology Transfer for Rural Areas, the national sustainable agriculture information center.

### Basic Organic Potting Mix

- 6 gallons sphagnum peat moss*
- ¼ cup lime (preferrably dolomite)
- 4.5 gallons vermiculite

## Potting Mix from Garden Soil

University of Hawai'i Cooperative Extension Service recommends that garden soil be tested before adding fertilizer, lime, or sulphur as needed. Be aware that using unsterilized garden soil increases the chances of your container planting becoming affected by soil-borne pests and diseases. Many gardeners like adding garden soil to potting mix when growing vegetables. UH suggests the following amounts when using garden soil in container gardens.

- 7 parts compost or good garden soil
- 2 parts organic matter (peat, well-rotted leaf mold)
- 1 part well-rotted manure
- 2 parts black sand or cinder ⅛ inch or less in diameter
- Treble superphosphate or bone meal (phosphorus), 2-3 pounds per cubic yard (2-3 tsp per 6-inch pot)
- Lime (dolomite), 2¼ pounds per cubic yard (2¼ tsp per 6-inch pot) to raise pH one unit
- Sulphur, 1 pound per cubic yard (1 tsp per 6-inch pot) to reduce pH one unit

You can add cinder or perlite to this mix to increase drainage. Call your local extension office to get information on having your soil tested. University of Hawai'i Cooperative Extension offices are listed at the back of this book.

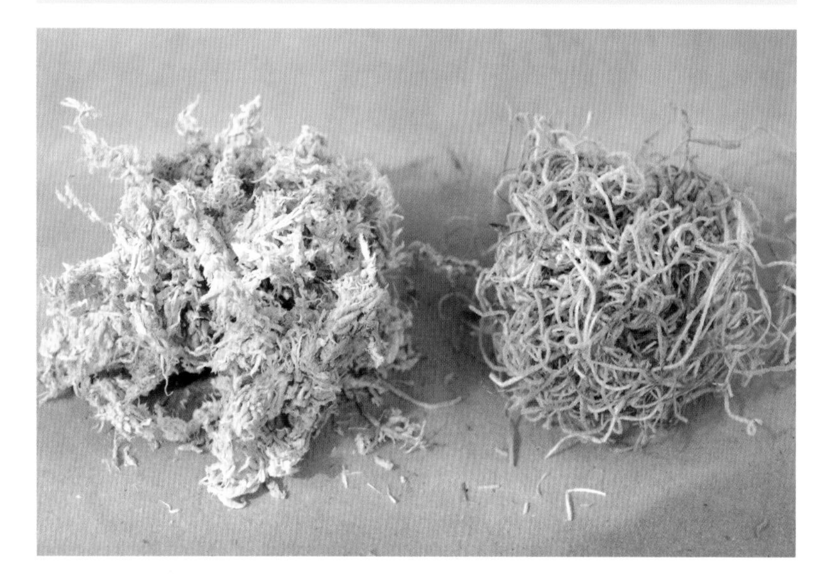

Sphagnum moss (left) is effective at retaining moisture. While it doesn't retain moisture as well, Spanish moss (right) is decorative and useful for concealing plastic pots that are double-potted.

- 4.5 gallons compost
- 1½ cups fertility mix made of:
  2 cups colloidal (rock) phosphate
  2 cups greensand*
  ½ cup bonemeal
  ¼ cup kelp meal

Blend well with water to moisten the mix.

*In Hawai'i, sphagnum peat moss and greensand can be expensive. Instead of using sphagnum moss, you can try experimenting with coir pith and dust, the short fibers that are left after the long coconut fibers are removed. Coir is commonly used in Europe and Australia. In a UH study of substitutions for peat in Hawai'i nursery production, coir was used to grow dwarf poinciana, and growth was equal to or better than that of peat. Composted green debris, composted municipal sewage waste, and composted macadamia nut husks also performed well. Of course that doesn't mean that all types of plants will have the same result, but you can give it a try. Instead of using greensand, try locally available medium blue rock sand from a building supplier that sells concrete and aggregates on your Island.

## MULCH

Mulch is a decorative layer with practical functions. Mulch keeps plants cool and slows evaporation. As mulches break down, they add nutrients and improve the structure of the potting mix. Coir chips, decorative bark or wood chips, and cinder are commonly used as mulch. Mulch that is available free from county green waste recycling programs is better if allowed to sit in a corner of the yard to decompose for a month or two before using. Composted macadamia nut husk is popular and more common on the Big Island.

A potting bench is ideal, but even an old desk from a thrift store or garage sale is a good workspace with convenient height and reach, plus storage.

## SETTING UP A WORKSPACE

Organize tools and materials in one convenient place. A greenhouse is ideal and you can build a potting bench, but you don't have to have anything fancy. Anything that allows you to work at waist level will do, such as sawhorses and plywood. Check thrift stores and garage sales for an old folding table, a discarded desk, or even a reusable ironing board. I use an old plywood desk I found at a thrift store for $10. A black plastic utility tub, the kind used to mix mortar, works well for mixing potting mix. Look for one in garden shops or the masonry section of hardware and home improvement stores. A wheelbarrow is helpful for mixing large quantities.

A garden trowel is useful for mixing media and filling pots. A small whiskbroom or brush makes it easy to sweep up the work surface in a jiffy. Five-gallon buckets, measuring spoons and cups, a watering can, pruners, and gloves are indispensable. For pest control, a mini pressure sprayer lets you mix small quantities of insecticidal soap and other home garden remedies. It sprays a fine mist more efficiently and with less effort than a typical spray bottle.

Keep fertilizers, potting mix, and other media in watertight plastic tubs and garbage cans so they stay free from contaminants. Buy scoops or make some by cutting up plastic laundry detergent bottles. Make labels using china markers or pencils and plastic plant tags, either purchased or recycled from cut-up plastic yogurt cups and discarded mini blinds. Stash a notebook and pencil close at hand, and hang a calendar to keep track of planting and fertilizing dates. You might even want to keep a garden diary: Take before and after photos, and keep records of blooming and fruiting times, what potting mix worked well, and so on.

In this arrangement, color families blend together in analogous hues of magenta, purple, and blue. For dramatic punch, use complementary colors such as yellow and violet, which are opposite each other on a color wheel.

## WHAT SHOULD YOU GROW?

### Determine Your Conditions

In the long run, if you match your plants to your growing conditions you'll have healthier growth and will spend less time troubleshooting. Before selecting plants, assess the conditions of the location you have chosen for growing.

### Growing Conditions Checklist

- How many hours of light does your lanai or patio receive?
- Is it in full sun, indirect sun, partial shade, or deep shade?
- Are there buildings, trees, or other structures that cast shadows during certain times of the day?
- Do shadows fall only in certain areas? Where?
- Is there exposure to salt spray or wind?
- Are your conditions usually dry, or does it tend to be humid and rainy?

Depending on the time of year, the angle of the sun will change and the amount of light may vary. Under unobstructed conditions, locations with southern exposure receive the most light and heat from the sun, and northern exposures receive less. East-facing areas have bright morning sun and shade in the afternoon, and west-facing ones have bright afternoon sun. If you live near the ocean, your plants might have to be tolerant of salt spray and trade winds that blow in from the northeast. If you are unsure of your conditions, it's easiest to start with tough plants that can tolerate some dryness, do well in full sun but are also shade tolerant.

### Select a Color Scheme

Under the Hawai'i sun, colors are brighter, bolder. Vivid hues and contrasts are hallmarks of the tropical garden. Harmonize colors within the same family of colors, located adjacent to each other on an artist's color wheel. Or pair up complementary colors, the ones that are opposite each other on a color wheel. For example, lively lime green and deepest burgundy make a stunning visual presentation. Some gardeners like to make a kalakoa quilt of many colors for a wild, lively look. Others

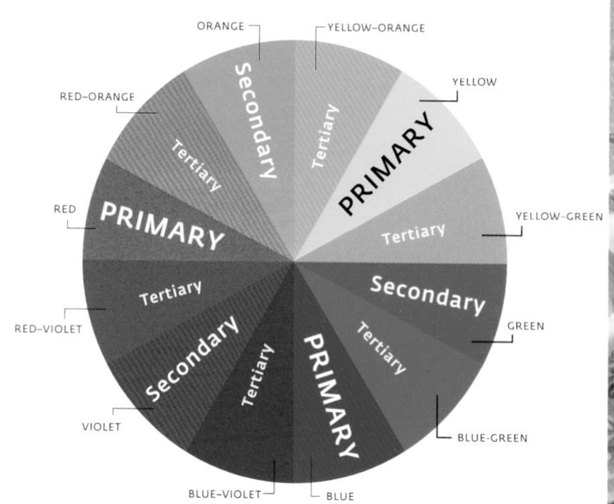


like to collect plants of one striking, unusual color, such as hybrids that have flowers or foliage of nearly black or chocolate brown.

Color sets the mood for your garden. Observe how color affects the way you feel about the interior of your home. It's likely you will enjoy a similar feeling in your exterior landscape. Traditional Japanese-style gardens typically feature a soothing, peaceful atmosphere of monochromatic green. White flowers feel light and refreshing in the daytime, and on a lanai at night they catch the moonlight. Plants with silver-gray, variegated, or shiny foliage stand out dramatically against dark backgrounds in night gardens or where shady areas need brightening.

Experiment with plants of different heights, textures, shapes, and hues to come up with novel combinations. A gardener in Kula, Maui, planted this astonishing tapestry of neon bright and smoky shades in a 24-inch coir-lined metal basket. Included here are New Zealand flax (*Phormium* hybrid), red spurge (*Euphorbia cotinifolia*), zinnia (*Zinnia*), marigold (*Tagetes*), bloodleaf (*Iresine herbstii*), purple basil (*Ocimum basilicum*), coleus (*Coleus x hybridus*), sweet potatoes (*Ipomoea batatas*), and spider plant (*Chlorophytum comosum*).

## Vary the Heights, Layer Your Plantings

Whether you are planting a combination garden in a single pot or placing several individual containers together, consider the scale of the planting in relation to the surrounding area. Varying heights adds visual interest and engages the viewer. You can think of your garden as a reflection of nature. In a forest, there are stories of vegetation: Trees make up the canopy, smaller trees and shrubs compose the understory, and the smallest plants ramble and cover the forest floor. In a basic garden design, a tall plant can lead the eye to a focal point in the middle of the arrangement. The middle layer should have some eye-catching feature, such as strong color. Trailing and low-growing plants draw the eye downward, making the connection with the earth.

Container gardens are often composed of plants that are not fully mature, and not all plants grow at the same rate. In combination plantings, plants can catch up to each other within the container and the plants can become all the same height. This is especially true in Hawai'i, where plants

Purple Persian-shield (*Strobilanthes dyerianus*) and burgundy New Guinea impatiens (*Impatiens hawkeri*) are the tall players. Asparagus fern (*Asparagus densiflorus*) fills in midheight with feathery green foliage, and oval-leaved creeping wirevine (*Muehlenbeckia*) tumbles over the side of a contrasting mustard-yellow pot.

known as annuals elsewhere go without the interruption of a cold winter and continue to grow as perennials. However, the resulting jumble can be separated and repotted. You can maintain the proportions of combination plantings by pruning and pinching back to control growth. See Chapter 8 for more on maintaining your container garden.

## Mix and Match Shapes and Textures

Put together diverse shapes of foliage and flowers to heighten interest. Make use of contrast and repetition to emphasize textures within your design. Place round-shaped leaves next to long-bladed, grass-like foliage, broad shiny leaves against feathery and needle-like ones. A variety of large and small sizes of flowers and leaves contribute to an overall pleasing impression of the arrangement. When shopping for plants, gather them together in a shopping basket or on a bench and try out several different groupings to see how they play off each other. Think of it as a casting call, and you are the director of this show: select one plant to be the star, and then add two or three pots of one other plant to play the supporting roles. Or create strikingly different yet unified looks by using the same type of plant with variations in leaf shape and color, such as motley, heart-shaped caladiums, also known locally as kalo kalakoa.

## Designing a Combination Container Garden

It is easier to manage a single plant grown in its own individual container, but planting a combination of plants is great fun. Container gardening is an excellent way to do something creative and constructive, get fresh air, exercise, and relieve stress. Keep in mind the basic principles of good design, and with experience you will develop your own personal style that you can share with others. A container garden can be a thoughtful, one-of-kind gift that you customize for someone special.

When planting a combination garden, it's best to choose from plants that have the same light and watering requirements. Think of them as an ʻohana that will be sharing one happy home. Usually, a basic combination design places the tallest plant in the middle of the container, then works outward with midsize plants, followed by low, trailing plants closest to the rim, allowing them to sweep over the side. Or, if the container will be viewed only from the front, you can put the tallest plant in the back, place fillers for the middle, and then line the front end of the container with trailing plants. Designs that use only 3 to 5 different plants are easier to manage. A container at least 16 inches in diameter or larger will hold several plants and will adequately retain moisture.

Gather plants, container, potting mix, fertilizer, and a watering can. Fill the container one-third to halfway with potting mix.

To release the plant, position the stems between your fingers and turn the pot upside down. If the plant does not drop into the palm of your hand, tap the rim of the pot on a firm surface.

## PLANTING

### Nine Easy Steps

1. Assemble together potting mix, amendments if you plan to use them, fertilizer, trowel, planting containers, watering can, and plants. If planting only one plant, choose a container that is the next size up from the current one. Exception: Choose a bigger container if the plant is one that grows large quickly.

2. If you are using an unglazed clay pot, presoak it in water for 30 minutes or even overnight in a bucket or a tub. Even a short soak of a few minutes or spraying it will help prevent it from wicking too much water away from the potting mix of the new planting.

3. Prepare potting mix, adding amendments if desired. Add water to the mix if it is too dry, and blend with a trowel. The potting mix should be moist and light, not clumpy or sludgy. Take care not to add too much water or the potting mix can compact, which could lead to drainage problems.

4. There is no need to add broken pottery shards or rocks for drainage. Scientific research shows potting mix actually drains better without them. If you want to improve drainage, mix in more perlite or cinder with the potting mix. If the drainage hole is too large, some gardeners use a bit of window screen, hardware cloth, or small pebbles to partially cover the drain hole. Don't use screen that is too fine or it might impede the flow of water.

5. Fill a container halfway with potting mix and check for the right height by placing the plant into the pot without removing it from its original plastic nursery pot. The surface of the media surrounding the base of the plant should be approximately at the same level when planted. Don't plant too deep.

6. Be sure the plant's roots are moist before removing them from the nursery pot. Support the plant with your open hand as you turn it upside down, positioning the stem between your index and middle fingers

Loosen the roots, carefully pulling them apart. If roots are bound, you can use pruners to carefully make a few vertical cuts around the bottom.

After firming the potting mix around the plants, topdress with a slow-release fertilizer if not already added to the mix. Place mulch around the base of the plant to cover the potting mix.

Pau! Except one last step: Place it in the right location for optimum growth, then water the planting thoroughly until it drains from the bottom.

if necessary. If the plant does not slide easily from the nursery pot, tap the upside-down rim on a table to release the plant. You can also use a knife to dislodge the roots from the inner sides of the nursery pot.

7. Gently loosen the roots. If the plant roots are tightly bound, carefully use pruners or a knife to make a few evenly spaced cuts at the bottom to help free the roots.

8. Place the plant in the pot and check its height within the pot once more. After you have loosened the roots, you might discover you have to add more potting mix to get the correct level. The plant should sit about 1 to 2 inches below the rim of the container, depending on the size of the container. This space between the potting mix surface and the container rim will act as a basin that fills at watering time. If you want to use decorative mulch such as bark or cinder, leave additional space at the top of the container to accommodate it.

9. Fill the remaining spaces around the plant with more potting mix. You can use a trowel, but your bare hands are easier to slip around leaves and stems without damaging them.

Press the potting mix firmly but gently around the plant, settling it in. Do not compact the mix or it could develop drainage problems. Topdress the planting with a slow-release fertilizer, following manufacturer's directions. Water thoroughly until water drains from the bottom of the container. Cover potting mix with mulch and moisten it.

## Planting Combination Gardens

Planting a combination garden is as simple as planting an individual plant, with a few more steps.

1. Start the same way by filling a container about halfway with potting mix. Estimate the proper height.

2. After loosening the roots, place the tallest plant in the container and check for the proper height, adding or removing potting mix beneath the plant as necessary.

3. Do the same for the smaller plants,

filling in spaces with potting mix as you go along, keeping the original level of the transplants. Usually you work outward from the center.

4. Gently press down the potting mix, making sure the surface of the potting mix is level throughout the container, allowing a 1-inch to 2-inch space from the top of the rim. There is no need to mulch a combination planting since the goal is to grow the plants close together to fill and overflow the container. Water your new combo planting until it drains from the bottom.

In the photos, a slightly different approach was used. Canna lilies are strong players and provide the focal point in this planting. After the canna lily was planted in the center, the trailing plants were settled in next to the rim. The remaining spaces in the container were filled in with native kupukupu fern.

## What Makes a Good Container Plant?

Almost any plant can be grown in a container. Most plants you buy from a nursery are already in a pot. The ultimate query is, what do want to keep in a pot and how much time, energy, and money are you willing to invest? If you know the mature height of the plant, you have some idea of how big your container will eventually have to be. Sometimes folly is obvious. A lychee tree, for example, will outgrow any container before it pays off with fruit. A plant that quickly outgrows a pot is more trouble than it is worth. Plants that need the company of many of the same type of plants for successful pollination, such as corn, probably won't provide a worthwhile harvest for the effort. You can grow ginger and heliconia in pots but you will have to divide them more often than ones planted in the ground. Some ornamentals such as pīkake

Fill the container partially with potting mix. Place the tallest plant, still in its nursery pot, into the container. Adjust the amount of potting mix to position the plant at the approximate height.

Plant trailing plants outermost, next to the rim.

Put midsized fillers between the tallest plant and the low trailing ones.

can get scrawny in pots but regular pruning can keep them compact. A mountain apple tree will fruit even when young, but it will require moving up to larger pots as it grows. Eventually it will be better to plant it in the ground. Other plants that would normally get big, such as certain palms, will remain small if grown in containers. Some native Hawaiian plants, including ʻōhiʻa lehua, can be kept in large pots for years. There are always exceptions. Explore Chapters 5 and 9 for plants recommended for Hawaiʻi container gardens. If you're adventurous and like to experiment, you could discover success with something new.

(above): In this garden, Heliconia grew in an old-fashioned aluminum cooking pot alongside variegated ornamental ginger (*Alpinia*) in a blue glazed pot.

Bold red-orange Canna lily (*Canna*) with deep purple foliage takes center stage. Native kupukupu fern (*Nephrolepis cordifolia*) and trailing 'Walkabout Sunset' (*Lysimachia congestiflora*) take supporting roles in this combo.

After a few weeks, plants fill out even more and recover with full bloom.

# 3 Island Landscapes in Small Spaces

## ENTRYWAYS WITH ISLAND STYLE

The prevailing way of life in the Islands is to welcome family, friends, and visitors to your home with aloha, to make them feel comfortable and at ease. Eye-catching container plantings invite people to your home with the message that you want to share the living beauty of Hawai'i. Bright colors, especially red, orange, and yellow, attract people and lead them up the driveway, up the stairs and to your doorstep. For instance, a tall ti plant

(above): A metal hayrack planter lined with coir and filled with blazing red angel-wing hybrid begonias (*Begonia coccinea*) accents the front of this house.

(right): These ti plants (*Cordyline fruticosa*) bring back fond memories for a retired Waimea rancher who brought cuttings with her when she moved to her home in Hilo. To control the growth of the ti plants, she planted them in containers. Tall, bright magenta ti plants contrast with the sky-blue exterior of this home and draw the eye toward a stairway leading to an entrance.

(above): A collection of bonsai on a porch is a calming, welcoming sight. The skylight above the porch lets in bright, filtered light for plants. A roll-up shade protects one side of the porch from the elements and adds privacy.

(right): Containers of various shapes, colors, and heights grouped according to a theme look balanced instead of cluttered.

with strong sculptural lines and flame-red foliage commands attention.

If you want something less flashy yet impressive, sentinels of groomed palms, assorted bonsai, and topiary set a formal tone, conveying an atmosphere of balance and calm. Use a row of container plantings of the same kind and uniform height to create a guide for visitors to follow to an entrance that is obscured from the driveway or street, or along areas where you want to establish barriers or screens.

Plants next to a walkway or entrance should not be so large that visitors have to maneuver around them or brush against them. To make guests feel welcome, avoid using plants with prickles, thorns, or long, spiky leaves. Many Hawai'i homeowners follow the tradition of growing ti plants around the perimeter to ward off bad luck. This is an attractive way to mark a boundary and provide a visual line to follow.

Avoid using too many random small pots, which can seem cluttering and distracting unless they are grouped by theme. For instance, a collection of Asian-inspired pottery holding your favorite shade-loving plants and orchids makes an elegant arrangement.

Remember, the entrance to your home makes the first impression. Give your home curb appeal by keeping container plantings healthy and maintained. Pick off dead leaves and blossoms, and replace diseased, infested, and dying plants as soon as possible.

## Fragrant Greetings

Ginger, pīkake, plumeria, pua kenikeni. What memories come to mind? Perhaps weddings, May Day celebrations, baby lūʻau, graduations, hula recitals, and airport farewells. Fragrance is a gentle Island greeting, and it can be a powerful part of a memory. Make your home a memorable

(above): Orchids make a spectacular display on a table and in a decorative wall-mounted hayrack planter lined with coir. Good air circulation is essential to growing healthy orchids.

(left): A tall, solitary urn with strong vertical form has dramatic visual impact at this entrance. Trailing plants drape over the sides, accentuating the shape.

Like the standard plumerias it needs full sun, but it stays low and shrubby. The soft pink and white blossoms have a light lemony scent. Dwarf gardenia, (*Gardenia augusta* 'Radicans'), is a petite version of its larger cousins. There is also a variegated form. These gardenias have a scent like the bigger varieties, but the leaves are dainty and as container plants they grow only 1 to 2 feet tall.

(above left): Colors and elongated oval shapes are repeated in this arrangement of white and green Stromanthe (*Stromanthe sanguinea* 'Tricolor') and Chinese furnishings.

(above right): *Kwai fah*, Chinese Sweet Olive (*Osmanthus fragrans*)

(right): An upended pot is an inexpensive, attractive plant stand.

place to visit with sweet-scented plants that are easy to grow in containers. Try pīkake, tuberose, and *kwai fah,* also known as Chinese sweet olive. Place fragrant plants such as maile-scented laua'e fern along pathways so that they release their scent when visitors brush past them. When fragrantly blooming plants are in containers, you can move them to under your bedroom window to enjoy their perfume at nighttime, too. Conversely, if your guests are sensitive to strongly scented plants, it's easy to relocate conainer plantings when necessary

If you like the look of plumeria but don't have much space, try a hybrid dwarf Singapore plumeria (*Plumeria obtusa*).

## DEFINING SPACE ON PATIO OR LANAI

Pots marching in straight lines on a patio or lanai work as barriers, but to create an area where guests want to linger you should arrange several coordinated groups of containers near sitting areas. Place plants at different heights to create interest by using plant stands, or something as simple as an overturned clay pot, a stack of bricks, or concrete blocks. Keep containers out of the way of foot traffic so that people feel at ease.

Repetition of colors, textures, and shapes of containers bring a group together, and variation keeps it exciting. Round up several pots of different sizes and finished with the same glaze. Or create a collection of bright white to antique white containers in clay or plastic for a refreshing look. Repetition can also be achieved with flowers and foliage in the same color family, such as a range of pink and white flowers teamed with variegated foliage.

## HYPERTUFA, HAWAIʻI STYLE

In ye old days of England, troughs that held water for livestock were carved out of a type of rock called tufa. Today's gardeners have transformed these weathered troughs into rustic planters. While it is next to impossible to obtain these in Hawaiʻi, you can make a lightweight substitute out of an easy-to-mold substance called hypertufa. It's an excellent way to reuse leftover perlite and vermiculite after rooting cuttings. Try making it on a weekend when you don't mind getting messy and you can invite some friends to join in. All you need to get started are a couple of free hours, some inexpensive materials, and a shady spot to set up a worktable.

### To make hypertufa, you'll need:

***Tools***

- Plastic sheeting to cover the worktable
- Safety goggles
- Dust mask
- Heavy-duty waterproof gloves
- Large plastic tub or wheelbarrow for mixing mortar
- Masonry trowel
- Large black plastic garbage bag
- Wire brush
- Flat head screwdriver
- Coarse wood file

***Materials***

- Portland cement (sold as "Hawaiian Cement, Type I-II")

Black-cinder hypertufa with *Carex wahuensis*, a native Hawaiian sedge. The rounded rim of this container was added after it was cured. Red dirt was rubbed on as a stain and washed off later for a more natural look. Natural lava rocks from the backyard were used as pot feet.

This simple hypertufa trough was molded with cardboard boxes. After it was leached and cured for one month, the trough was filled with a well-draining potting mix high in perlite. Then it was planted with shallow-rooted, slow-growing succulents. Store-bought gray bricks were used as pot feet, but you can also make your own using leftover hypertufa material.

- Peat, sifted
- Perlite

  *You can use other kinds of aggregates, such as:*
- Vermiculite
- Builder's sand (not beach sand)
- Crushed cinder or gravel, ½ inch in diameter or smaller
- Optional: Concrete coloring

A good rule of thumb is to use **1 part Portland cement to 3 parts of aggregate.** Portland cement is cement only, not concrete mix. No sand or other aggregate has been added to it. It usually comes in a 94-pound bag. (Yes, take a buddy to help you pick up materials.) Go to a masonry supplier to get reinforcing fiber, sometimes referred to in the trade by a brand name, Fibermesh. Perlite and peat make hypertufa lighter than concrete. You can achieve different looks with other materials such as builder's sand, vermiculite, or gravel, but the result is likely to be heavier. Peat should be sifted before using to eliminate lumps and remove stems.

### Instructions for a Trough

For this project I used these proportions.

- 2 gallons Portland cement
- 3 gallons perlite
- 3 gallons peat, sifted
- 1 small handful of reinforcing fiber for concrete
- Water

To make a small trough from cardboard boxes you need two boxes (a small one that fits inside a larger one). Check to make sure there will be 2 to 3 inches of space between them on all sides.

Before you begin, put on your safety gear. Wear waterproof gloves, goggles, and a dust mask. Cement is highly caustic, and your hands can get dried out and sore in no time. You definitely don't want to get any in your eyes or lungs.

Cement, peat, and reinforcing fibers blow around even in a slight breeze, so put them into your mixing tub first, followed by the heavier materials on top, in this case the perlite.

Combine the dry ingredients a bit, and then gradually add water. You can mix with a trowel but I do a more thorough job by squishing and kneading the material with gloved hands. Use only enough water to make the material moldable. That is, the mixture should be just moist enough so that you can squeeze a handful of material into a decent ball that releases just a few drops of water. Too much water results in a "slumpy" mix that won't hold its shape and cures into a weak container with a tendency to crack.

Put a 2- to 3-inch layer of the hypertufa material in the bottom of the larger box. Pat it down evenly.

After creating the bottom layer, place the smaller box inside the larger one. Evenly fill in the space between them with material, pressing out any air pockets. If the inner box starts collapsing you can put sand or cinder in it to keep it rigid.

When you have filled the space to create the height you want, level off the top edges.

## Curing Hypertufa

Slow curing makes a strong container. Cover your project with the plastic garbage bag to keep it moist and prevent it from cracking while it cures for the first 24 to 36 hours. Do not move it, as it is fragile at this stage. Check on it periodically to see if it is set enough. It should be firm but soft enough to carve into with a screwdriver. If it's set, tear off the wet cardboard and begin shaping the trough.

To make the trough look less boxy, round off the corners with a coarse wood file. Use the wire brush to rough up the surface. Distress the surface even more, if desired, by scratching some grooves into the sides using a screwdriver.

Now you're ready for the final cure. Leave your hypertufa creation in the shade for a month or longer to harden and cure fully. Cement has a lot of lime in it, and too much is toxic to plants, so you will need to leach it out before planting. For a couple of weeks, fill the trough with water and let it soak for for a few hours, then empty and rinse it out. If you live in a rainy place, keeping it under a shady tree to cure is ideal.

When it is fully cured, drill holes in the bottom of the container using a ½-inch diameter masonry bit. If the container looks "hairy" with fibers sticking out, burn them off with a small propane torch.

A) Add water a little at a time, mixing after each addition of water. Too much water makes the hypertufa material difficult to work with and weakens the container.

B) Squeeze a handful of material to see if it produces a few drops of water.

C) The material should be moldable, something like bumpy wet clay. Form it into a ball to see if it holds its shape well.

D) After forming the bottom layer, place the smaller box into the larger box. Put sand into the inner box if it looks like the sides might start collapsing.

E) When the desired height is reached, pat down and level the rim. Cover with a plastic bag and cure for 24 to 36 hours. After the initial cure, remove the cardboard.

F) Carefully shape and texturize the container. Try not to handle the container too much in this early stage. After a couple of weeks, leach by filling the container with water and letting it sit a few hours before pouring it out. Let cure for at least a month before planting.

C

D

E

F

## More Hyper Ideas

You can make other shapes using plastic dishes, flowerpots, cooking pans, and other containers. Instead of using two molds, you use just one, forming the material on the outside of a mold turned upside down. Plastic molds won't stick to cement, but ones of wood, clay, and metal will, so cover them with a plastic bag before using. Then you will be able to release the mold easily after the initial cure. Make sure the folds of the bag lie flat. Folds that get deeply embedded into the hypertufa material will, in effect, make a crack that weakens the container.

To make a bowl-shaped planter, use a plastic bowl. Turn it upside down and begin by molding material at the edge resting against the table surface. Form a 1½- to 2-inch thick layer, pressing firmly to make it strong. You can check the thickness of the walls by sticking in a wooden chopstick. Don't forget to press out the puka after checking.

Work your way up, covering the bottom of the inverted mold last. Level off what will be the bottom of the hypertufa container if you want it to sit on a flat surface without rocking.

To eliminate the need for drilling later, you can make drainage holes at this point. Make a puka in the wet hypertufa with a ½-inch diameter dowel. If the hole closes up slightly, you can carve it open with a screwdriver when you remove the mold after the first cure.

After the final month-long cure, you can age hypertufa with the same method used for clay pots, using a coating of buttermilk or yogurt and ground-up moss (Chapter 2). Hypertufa improves with age: The longer it sits, the stronger it gets.

Hypertufa containers are great for herb gardens, succulents, and cacti. Gardeners in temperate regions like to use them for alpine gardens, but here the natural appearance of hypertufa can nicely set off native Hawaiian plants. With hypertufa you can

*(continued on page 38)*

To use a plastic bowl, start forming the material from the edge that meets the table. Work upward, adding enough material to make the walls about 2 inches thick. Use a chopstick or dowel to check the thickness.

## Coral Sand Recipe

A light-colored, smoother, sandy hypertufa reminiscent of the beach. Heavier than the basic recipe.

- 2 gallons Portland cement
- 3 gallons peat
- 1 gallon vermiculite
- 2 gallons purchased coral sand from builder's supplier
- 1 small handful of reinforcing fiber for concrete
- Water

The two containers at left were made with coral sand hypertufa. At right, black cinder hypertufa.

make containers according your specific needs, and many native Hawaiian plants, especially coastal ones, need shallow, broad containers. Be creative and come up with your own Island-style designs. Experiment with concrete dyes, crushed red or black cinder. You can try embedding beach glass or shells on the outer surface but these additions should be washed free of salts that can inhibit the setting of concrete. Don't use beach sand, however. It's too full of small bits of material that can interfere with a strong cure. Instead, purchase clean, washed coral sand or basaltic sand specifically intended for mixing with concrete.

## Black Cinder Recipe

Darker gray, bumpy lava rock-like hypertufa.

- 2 gallons Portland cement
- 2 gallons peat
- 1 gallon vermiculite
- 1 gallon black cinder, crushed to ¼ inch diameter and smaller
- 2 gallons basaltic sand (sometimes sold as "termite barrier")
- 1 small handful of reinforcing fibers
- Black concrete coloring, mixed with enough water

Black cinder is similar to perlite in that it is lightweight, but as it weathers it shows up blackish brown instead of white. Use a hammer to crush cinder to a workable size. Too much cinder or too much added coloring will cause hypertufa to crumble. For a weathered Hawaiian rock-like appearance, rub on moist red dirt, which is high in iron oxides, after the month-long cure. Let it dry for a few days, and then rinse it off.

# 4 Creating a High-rise Paradise

'Awa (*Piper methysticum*) and native hāpu'u tree fern (*Cibotium*) on a balcony with afternoon shade.

Apartments and high-rises often have rules regarding plants on lanais. Even if they don't, it makes sense to take measures to prove that your private oasis won't cause problems for neighbors living below you or next door. Treat your plants on the lanai as though they were on a carpet indoors. Use saucers to catch water runoff. Use a container without holes as a cachepot to hold a smaller pot that drains water. Be a good neighbor, and show your aloha. It's common sense to empty runoff water into a drain indoors, not over the railing.

## LIGHTWEIGHT PLANTING

Several large pots of well-watered potting mix can add up to a heavy load on a balcony. If you want to reduce the weight of your container garden, use lightweight containers and make a lighter potting mix. If you are using a store-bought potting mix, add one part perlite to two parts potting mix. This mix will dry out quickly, so water more frequently and use water-retaining strategies.

## PREVENTING EVAPORATION

To prevent rapid evaporation, try using plastic or foam containers. Large containers retain water better than small ones. Grouping pots together also helps plants stay moist. Mulch is the best friend of the container gardener. Cinder, mulch (store-bought or from a recycling center), or even a layer of compost will do a better job at retaining moisture than wood chips. Although polymer (right): Bamboo can screen and soften a view, and its leaves make a pleasant, soft rustling sound.

crystals are touted as a way to retain and make water available to plants in dry conditions, in scientific tests it gets mixed results. When water is added to polymer crystals, they double in size and become globs of gel. The gel is then supposed to be incorporated into potting mix or soil. Manufacturers claim that plant roots will seek water stored in the gel when conditions become dry. Whether the roots actually do this isn't certain, and some people find that the gel doesn't seem to make a huge difference. Also, gels can simply retain too much water within the potting mix and cause the plant to rot. You are probably better off spending your money on mulch and other proven water-retaining measures.

## COMPLEMENTING OR SCREENING A VIEW

Living in a high-rise can yield some spectacular views of the mountains and shorelines. For many urban dwellers, seeing the landscape is an inspiring way to begin or end the day. Morning mists envelope lush green valleys, fiery sunsets ebb into the shimmering sea, leaving behind a twinkling, humming cityscape. If your view is a desirable one, complementing it is a simple matter of echoing what you see. Get clues for what thrives in your area by looking at what is being kept in containers in public places near you, in street planters, and in plantings at shopping centers and resorts. Also check out nearby yards and gardens.

But what if your view is uninspiring? Make your own paradise. Grow vines on trellises to screen offending scenery and to create privacy. If your balcony is not too high up and windy, you can also use tall plants to screen. Try dracaena for shady areas and bamboo in full sun or indirect light. Anchor a tall plant to keep it from toppling over in the event a gust of wind should kick up. Tie it to a post or railing if possible.

(above): Ti plant *(Cordyline fruticosa)*, *Syngonium*, and asparagus fern *(Asparagus densiflorus)*, cascades from a street planter.

Dracaena 'Janet Craig' makes an effective screen on a lanai with partial shade. Tall plants in windy areas should be tied to a support or fastened to a wall.

## TROPICAL VINES FOR CONTAINERS

Each of these vines have showy or fragrant flowers and can be used as a living screen if trained to a trellis set in a large container on a balcony, lanai, or patio. Prune regularly to shape and to encourage flowering and fuller growth.

Pink mandevilla vine (*Mandevilla x amabilis*) adds an uplifting splash of color while screening a balcony or lanai. Another popular variety is large-flowered 'Alice du Pont'. Mandevilla is semidormant during winter; new growth appears in early spring.

| NAME<br>***Botanical name*** | LIGHT | NOTES |
|---|---|---|
| ʻĀwikiwiki<br>*Canavalia galeata* | Full sun | Striking deep purple blossoms. Native to Waiʻanae mountains. |
| Bougainvillea<br>*Bougainvillea* | Full sun | Salt, wind tolerant. No high nitrogen fertilizers/overwatering. |
| Bower Vine<br>*Pandorea jasminoides* | Full sun | White to light pink flowers bloom fall to spring. |
| Butterfly Pea<br>*Clitoria ternatea* | Full sun, partial shade | Blue or white flowers bloom in summer. |
| Confederate Jasmine<br>*Jasminum laurifolium* forma *nitidum* | Full sun, partial shade | Salt tolerant. Fragrant white flowers nearly year-round. |
| Kūhiō Vine<br>*Ipomoea horsfalliae* | Full sun, indirect sun | Deep pink flowers bloom almost year-round. |
| Mandevilla<br>*Mandevilla x amabilis* | Full sun | White, light pink to magenta flowers bloom spring to fall. |
| Orchid Vine<br>*Stigmaphyllon floribundum* | Full sun, partial shade | Yellow flowers bloom spring to fall. |
| Pakalana<br>*Telosma cordata* | Full sun | Fragrant greenish-yellow flowers bloom May to summer. |
| Nanea<br>*Vigna marina* | Full sun | Bright yellow-green flowers. Native to Hawaiʻi's beaches. |
| Stephanotis<br>*Marsdenia floribunda* | Full sun | Heat, salt tolerant. Fragrant flowers bloom winter to spring. |

(above): Succulents, cacti, and other desert plants require little care and brighten a hot, dry lanai or sunny porch in leeward areas. Use a potting mix high in perlite or cinder and allow it to dry between waterings to prevent rot. Keep plants under shelter during periods of heavy rain.

(right): Malabar chestnut (*Pachira aquatica*) is easy to care for as bonsai, and it tolerates a range of light from full sun to partial shade.

## OVEREXPOSED CONDITIONS

Apartment balconies and patios can be hot, dry, and windy. If these are your conditions, use water-retaining strategies and select plants that tolerate wind and heat. If you live by the ocean, your plants should also stand tough against salty air. Too much wind rules out hanging baskets. Plants adapted to desert conditions, such as succulents and cacti, can be dazzling when in bloom, and they pay off with low maintenance.

## SHADY CONDITIONS

Plants that aren't receiving enough sunlight become pale and spindly with underdeveloped leaves. If your balcony has a wall that casts the floor in shadow, place plants higher up so that they receive better light exposure. Use wire or plastic shelving, or use a plant stand. Grow shade-tolerant plants if your lanai receives less than 4 hours of full sun per day. Plants that receive more light from one direction will grow lopsided. Give plants a quarter-turn every so often so that they fill out more evenly.

## MASKING NOISE

Create a backdrop of soothing sound with your garden. While they won't shut out a neighbor's blaring stereo, plants such as bamboo and potted palms have leaves that rustle in the breeze. Tall plants with large round leaves can help deflect noise. The gentle trickling of a tabletop fountain can add another layer of sound to block out noise from city streets. Indoors, a quiet fan or air conditioner and soft music can wash over a noisy background with a more peaceful atmosphere.

## INTERIOR GARDENS

The best interior plants are shade tolerant. When purchasing plants for indoors, notice where they are kept in the nursery where you are purchasing them. Are they under shade or in full sun? If the plant is being kept in full sun it might not

(left): Polka-dot begonia (*Begonia maculata*) needs filtered light and high humidity.

(below): Water trickles peacefully over this simple indoor fountain of Hawaiian pōhaku (stone) and laua'e fern (*Microsorum scolopendria*). Although it seems to have a lot of water circulating and it looks heavy, a shallow basin nested within the pot actually holds the stones and a small amount of water.

Some "snails" are nice to plants.

Judicious pruning keeps this indoor ivy in shape.

do well indoors under low-light conditions. Your best bet is to place interior plants near a window with indirect or filtered sunlight. If you've ever had sunburn after an all-day picnic, you know that it can happen before you notice. The same is true for plants. Be aware of possible overexposure if interior plants are moved to outdoors for even a short period. If your home is being tented for termites, instead of putting your interior plants outside in the blistering sun, ask someone to store them at their house in a shaded area.

Keep plants away from direct exposure to air conditioners, which are too cold and drying. Water as needed, usually once or twice a week. Remember to fertilize regularly with a slow-release fertilizer as directed by the manufacturer. Occasionally refresh the plant by rinsing off the dust. Set it under a shower of cool water, or wipe smooth, shiny leaves with a damp cloth. If you go on vacation with no one back home to take care of your houseplants, you can keep them in your bathroom for a week. Lay a sheet of plastic in the bathtub. Add layer of wet newspaper. Give the plants a good soak. Close the shower to keep in moisture.

What if you have to be away longer? You can keep houseplants moist for at least 2 weeks, possibly up to 30 days, with a water-gel. Though it isn't cheap, it is convenient and effective for interior plants. DriWater is a patented product that had been successfully used in restoring native vegetation in the arid terrain of Kaho'olawe. The gel provides new plantings with a supply of water while they are becoming established. You can use the smaller 2-inch diameter version for continuous watering of your indoor plants. The sausage-like capsule of gel is slit open and either placed on top of the moist potting mix or delivered through a tube. I tried one on a *Ficus benjamina* I kept indoors and undisturbed in an 8-inch pot. It was healthy for about 3 weeks and put out new growth. After four weeks, the leaves started to turn yellow and drop. After I flushed the potting mix with water, the plant eventually regained its health.

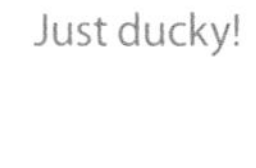

Just ducky!

## Common Problems of Indoor Plants

If you are unsure of the cause of the problem, contact your local cooperative extension office for a diagnosis and for recommendations of environment-friendly controls for home gardeners. See the resource section in Chapter 10 for contact information for the extension office nearest you.

| SYMPTOMS | POSSIBLE CAUSES | SOLUTIONS |
|---|---|---|
| Wilting, rot | Too much water<br>Too much fertilizer | Water once or twice a week. Remove standing water.<br>Flush out excess fertilizer. |
| Wilting, leaves turning brown at tips | Too little water<br>Too much fertilizer | Surface of media should be moist. Use self-watering container.<br>Flush out excess fertilizer. |
| Slow, stunted growth; yellowing | Lack of fertilizer<br>Overgrown in pot<br>Disease | Use slow-release fertilizer. Mark a reminder on your calendar.<br>Repot if necessary.<br>Contact local extension for advice. |
| Pale, tall, spindly growth; small leaves | Not enough light | Move near sunny window. Grow shade tolerant plants. |
| Leaves dropping | Exposure to air conditioning<br>Overwatering, root rot<br>Not enough light<br>Disease | Move plant away from vents.<br>Reduce watering.<br>Relocate for better light exposure.<br>Contact local extension for advice. |
| Leaves brown on the margins and tips | Fertilizer-salt buildup in potting media<br>Too little water | If your plant has been in its pot for over a year, and if the clay pot has a white crust on the outside, the media may be "burning" the leaves with leftover salts from fertilizers. Repot the plant by removing it from the pot and replacing old media with fresh media. Soak and scrub the pot before reusing.<br>Water regularly. |
| White fuzzy, waxy spots | Mealy bugs | Use eco-friendly controls. Handpick or spray with commercial or homemade insecticidal soap. Do not use soap on ferns. A strong shot of water can also knock off aphids from the plant. Gently scrape off scale, or brush with an old toothbrush to remove, then spray with insecticidal soap. Homemade remedy: Mix 1 tablespoon liquid soap (such as Dr. Bronner's from natural food store) with 1 gallon water. Use a spray bottle to treat affected areas. |
| Curling, stunted leaves; webs | Spider mites, broad mites | |
| Small barnacle-like black spots along leaf veins | Scale insects | |
| White-winged insects on underside of leaves | Whiteflies | |
| Tiny green insects on underside of leaves | Aphids | |

# 5 Popular Island Designs

## ASIAN PACIFIC INFLUENCES

Hawai'i's container gardens are accents to Island-style landscapes. Deeply rooted in the gardens of Hawai'i are the memories of Pacific and Asian experiences. Japanese gardens in Hawai'i feature plants that are cold-weather look-alikes, hybridizing the aesthetics of two worlds an ocean apart. Balinese themes connect the viewer to the earth with natural colors and textures. Polynesian "canoe plants" and pōhaku (stones) worn smooth by streams are part of the rich cultural and natural history of Hawai'i. In each garden is the expression of the inner landscape of its creator.

(above): Objects brought home from travels abroad give your garden personal meaning.

(left): Container plantings and sacred art integrate the lush layers of this garden.

**LAYERS** of container plantings complete a lush, tropical look. Place containers so that you create a graduated effect with shorter plants in front of taller plants.

**STONE** has visual weight and imparts a feeling of balance and stability.

(above left): Ornamental banana *(Musa)* takes center stage with layers of orchids, begonias, anthuriums, and other tropicals in pots.

(left): Dwarf Schefflera with a collection of small stones and other "found" objects.

(above): Hawaiian lava rock weathers from deep black to dark gray, sometimes reddish to yellowish brown. Smooth Hawaiian river pōhaku are native to local landscapes and look natural in Hawai'i gardens.

**WATER** is calming. Features such as small fountains, fish bowls, and water gardens play a meditative, tranquil note.

(above): A fountain kit for a half-barrel is a convenient way to make an Island-themed water garden for the lanai. Native neke fern (*Cyclosorus interruptus*) and Hawaiian kalo (*Colocasia esculenta*) have only their roots submerged. Potted native hāpu'u (*Cibotium*) and a young māmaki (*Pipturus albidus*) are placed behind the fountain in partial shade.

(left): In this arrangement, circular patterns echo each other. A tall, spiky plant behind the fountain bowl draws attention to the movement of the water.

**ART** can be a focal point in the garden. Include objects that inspire you at a glimpse and lighten your heart.

"Garden Goddesses" by Volcano artist Ira Ono watch over this container garden with purple-heart (*Tradescantia pallida* 'Purpurea'), Euphorbia, and Coleus (*Coleus x hybridus*).

Set a mood for your garden. Include pieces that are whimsical and cheerful . . .

. . . or quiet and restful. Cast concrete garden sculpture by artist Deborah Bridges.

## NATIVE HAWAIIAN PLANTS FOR CONTAINERS

Native Hawaiian plants have a serene beauty all their own. They are part of an ancient botanical history found nowhere else in the world. Although native plants tend to do better when planted in the ground, with enough care and attention many native plants are excellent container plants. In general, native plants need good drainage. Red or black volcanic cinders are naturally the best amendments to use to increase drainage of commercial potting mixes, which tend to have a high amount of water-retaining peat. For coastal natives, coral chips can be used instead of cinder. Coastal natives tend to do well in containers. They are usually shallow-rooted, tough plants that can withstand dry conditions, wind, and salt spray. Use half the amount of fertilizer, and use pesticides with caution if at all, as native plants can be very sensitive.

Some rain forest plants make good houseplants, such as ʻalaʻala wai nui, pāpala, pāpala kēpau, and ferns. Neke fern, a marshland plant, is perfect for water gardens. Obtain native plants from a friend or local nursery, and do not collect from the wild. Nursery owner Rick Barboza of Hui Ku Maoli Native Hawaiian Plant Specialists recommended the native plants listed here. They are usually available in local nurseries and are easy to grow. An excellent source of information on native plants for home gardens is *Growing Native Hawaiian Plants: A How-to Guide for the Gardener* by Heidi Bornhorst (Bess Press 2005).

(below left): Māmaki (*Pipturus albidus*)

(below right): ʻAlaʻala wai nui (*Peperomia*)

### Natives that Prefer Moist Conditions

These prefer moist conditions but can be grown in dry, hot leeward areas if given enough water and protection from the sun.

| HAWAIIAN NAME | BOTANICAL NAME (COMMON NAME) | LIGHT |
|---|---|---|
| ʻAlaʻala wai nui | *Peperomia spp.* | Shade, partial shade |
| ʻAeʻae | *Bacopa monnieri* (Water Hyssop) | Full to partial sun |
| Māmaki | *Pipturus albidus* | Partial shade |
| ʻŌhiʻa lehua | *Metrosideros polymorpha* | Full sun |
| Pāpala | *Charpentiera densiflora* | Partial shade |
| Pāpala kēpau | *Pisonia brunoniana* | Partial shade |
| ʻUkiʻuki | *Dianella sandwicensis* | Full sun to partial shade |
| ----- | *Munroidendron racemosum* | Full sun to partial shade |

## Natives that Prefer Dry Conditions

These require regular watering if planted in containers.

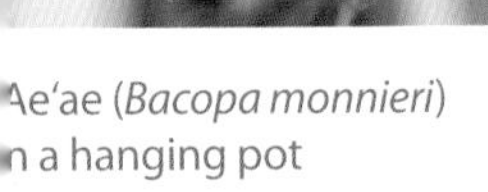

ʻAeʻae (*Bacopa monnieri*) in a hanging pot

ʻĀkia (*Wikstroemia uva-ursi*)

Ālula (*Brighamia*)

Pōhinahina (*Vitex rotundifolia*)

| HAWAIIAN NAME | BOTANICAL NAME (COMMON NAME) | LIGHT |
|---|---|---|
| ʻĀkia | *Wikstroemia uva-ursi* | Full sun |
| ʻAeʻae | *Bacopa monnieri* (Water Hyssop) | Full to partial sun |
| ʻĀkulikuli | *Sesuvium portulacastrum* | Full sun |
| Ālula | *Brighamia spp.* | Partial sun |
| Hinahina | *Heliotropium anomalum* | Full sun |
| ʻIhi | *Portulaca spp.* | Full sun |
| Koʻokoʻolau | *Bidens spp.* | Full sun to filtered sun |
| Kuluʻī | *Nototrichium sandwicense* | Full sun |
| Loulu | *Pritchardia spp.* | Full sun to partial shade |
| Maʻu ʻaki ʻaki | *Fimbristylis cymosa* | Full sun |
| Nanea | *Vigna marina* (Beach Pea) | Full sun |
| Naupaka kahakai | *Scaevola sericea* (Beach Naupaka) | Full sun |
| ʻOhai | *Sesbania tomentosa* | Full sun |
| Pāʻū-o-Hiʻiaka | *Jacquemontia ovalifolia* subsp. *sandwicensis* | Full sun |
| Pōhinahina | *Vitex rotundifolia* (Beach Vitex) | Full sun |
| ʻUki | *Machaerina angustifolia* | Full sun |
| ʻŪlei | *Osteomeles anthyllidifolia* | Full sun to partial sun |
| ----- | *Carex wahuensis* (Hawaiian sedge) | Full sun to partial sun |

## Native Ferns

Ferns need rich, well-draining potting mix. Most do well with a fish emulsion fertilizer. A little good garden soil added to the potting mix is also beneficial. They flourish on a lanai or patio with high humidity and shady conditions or partial sun. In dry areas outdoors, regular misting helps. Indoors, a sunlit bathroom is an ideal spot for ferns such as palapalai and ʻēkaha.

Kupukupu *(Nephrolepis cordifolia)*, native Hawaiian sword fern

Hāpu'u *(Cibotium)*, native Hawaiian tree fern

Ēkaha, Bird's nest fern (*Asplenium nidus*)

| HAWAIIAN NAME | BOTANICAL NAME (COMMON NAME) | LIGHT |
|---|---|---|
| ʻĒkaha | *Asplenium nidus* (Bird's Nest Fern) | Shade, indirect sun |
| Hāpuʻu | *Cibotium spp.* (Hawaiian Tree Fern) | Partial shade |
| Kupukupu | *Nephrolepis cordifolia* (Sword Fern) | Full or partial sun |
| Kupukupu (Pāmoho) | *Nephrolepis exaltata* (Sword Fern) | Full or partial sun |
| Palapalai | *Microlepia strigosa* | Bright indirect sun |
| Neke | *Cyclosorus interruptus* (Swamp Cyclosorus) | Full or partial sun |

'Ēkaha, closeup
(*Asplenium nidus*)

# 6 'Onolicious Edibles

Enjoy once more the sweetness of an 'ono pineapple (*Ananas comosus*) by planting the crown. The crown can be rooted in a cup of water first.

Growing your own food saves energy, is healthier for you, and is better for the environment. Vegetables and fruits in containers are more work and time-consuming than ornamentals, but the results can be deliciously satisfying. Keep potting mix moist by watering at least twice a day in warm, dry weather. In addition to a slow-release fertilizer at planting time, you must supplement with liquid fertilizer every week.

## LIGHT REQUIREMENTS

If your garden sits in morning or afternoon shadow, there might not be enough light to grow most fruits and vegetables. Unobstructed southern exposure will give you more success

A small worm bin allows even apartment and condo dwellers to make compost.

with edibles. However, even if you have only 4 hours of sun you can still grow lettuces and other greens that prefer some cool shade.

## GROWING ORGANICALLY

You can mix your own version of organic potting mix (See Chapter 2 for a basic do-it-yourself recipe) or go the fast and easy route by purchasing a premium organic potting mix. The types of materials used in potting mixes labeled as "organic" can vary quite a bit. Look for organic potting mixes that are labeled as OMRI-listed. OMRI, the Organic Materials Review Institute, is a nonprofit organization that provides the organic industry with guidance on suitability of materials according to USDA National Organic Program standards. These are products that are in compliance with USDA guidelines for certified organic production.

Smoky purple 'Uahi-a-Pele' Hawaiian taro (*Colocasia esculenta* 'Uahi-a-Pele') makes an excellent poi. Historically, this taro is important in Hawaiian culture as medicine and as an offering to the gods.

Edibles are usually heavy feeders, so it's a good idea to blend organic fertilizer with the potting mix for the initial planting. Some gardeners like to incorporate a bit of good garden soil as well. There are several commercially formulated granular organic fertilizers on the market. However, some gardeners still prefer to use the inexpensive old standby, aged chicken manure. To prevent transferring of diseases, be sure that any manures you use are **well-composted,** and be extra careful about using manures around edible greens. Combine 3 parts potting mix to 1 part **composted** chicken manure. Organic fertilizers break down slowly. To supplement, apply fish emulsion/seaweed fertilizer as directed by the manufacturer. I fertilize edibles with these amounts once a week.

1 gallon water
1 tablespoon fish emulsion
1 teaspoon seaweed extract

Apply fertilizer when it looks like the plant needs it, and only when the roots are moist. I use deodorized fish emulsion, which is still a little hauna. Dogs and cats sniff around it but don't seem to be much more interested than that. The odor disappears after a day or two. I don't foliar feed. I live on the windward side, and in warm, humid weather some plants are more susceptible to powdery mildew and other diseases if their leaves get wet. I have found better results when I use the fish emulsion/seaweed concoction as a drench, applying it directly to the potting mix. About 1 cup for each foot of plant height is enough.

If you don't have a yard for a full-blown compost pile, you still can keep a small worm bin for composting fruit and vegetable scraps. Sometimes listed on the label of commercially made organic potting mixes, earthworm castings are an excellent organic fertilizer to add to your container plantings. When done correctly, composting with worms is simple and nearly odorless. All you need are Hawai'i's own composting worms, a worm bin, some newspaper, compostable food scraps, and water. By composting with earthworms you'll be doing your part to reduce landfills and tapping into the nutrient cycle to grow healthy plants. Setting up and maintaining a worm bin is an excellent opportunity to teach children concepts in life sciences, too.

You can either make your own worm bin or order one locally. Ready-made worm bins for the home composter come in sizes small to large, for the apartment dweller on up. **It is illegal to import composting worms from outside the state of Hawai'i.** There are hefty fines that the state Department of Agriculture can impose on the supplier and the receiver of imported worms. Piper Selden, coauthor of UH publications on worm composting, said that Hawai'i's composting worm is a different species from the one in North America. Tropical composting worms eat more and make compost faster. Obtain them locally from a friend with an existing worm bin or order the worms from a reputable supplier within Hawai'i. Check with your local county extension office or recycling program for referrals to suppliers on your Island. Also shop around the state for the best deals. Raising worms in Hawai'i has some unique challenges, so seek the expertise of local worm suppliers who are most familiar with these problems and can inform you on the best techniques for worm composting in Hawai'i. A few are listed among the resources at the back of this book.

## SPACE-SAVING VEGETABLES AND FRUITS

If you are short on space, try growing dwarf and bush-type fruits and vegetables. However, some bush varieties of beans and cukes are less prolific, so sometimes it is better to plant climbing vines that you can train vertically. Use a layer of mulch or compost to keep roots cool and moist, and to provide nutrition as it breaks down. Fertilize organically, or if you prefer, add a synthetic slow-release fertilizer such as Osmocote or Nutricote to the planting mix.

(above): Plant pole string beans (*Phaseolus vulgaris*) in a barrel and train them to a trellis. Pick them while still young so that plants keep producing.

(left): Japanese eggplant 'Ichiban' (*Solanum melongena* 'Ichiban') is a prolific producer in a container.

*Free publications on home garden vegetables are available from the University of Hawai'i Cooperative Extension Service. Check their website for downloads at www.ctahr.hawaii.edu or call your local extension office.*

'Kung Pao' hot chile peppers (*Capsicum annuum* 'Kung Pao') from Thailand grow fast, can be used fresh, and are good for drying. Great for Thai, Szechuan, and Southeast Asian dishes.

## Vegetables & Fruits for Hawaiʻi Container Gardens

### W= Warm weather, C= Cool weather

| VEGETABLE/FRUIT | TYPE | CONTAINER | TIPS |
|---|---|---|---|
| Banana (*Musa acuminata*) (W) | Apple, also called Brazilian | 18" dia. or larger (10-15 gal.) barrel or tub | Doesn't always set fruit, but looks nice as an ornamental. Wind tolerant. Grows 8-10 ft. Keep moist. Heavy feeder. Prefers rich organic potting mix. |
| Citrus (W) | Improved Meyer lemon; Bearss or Tahitian lime; Calamondin | 18" dia. or larger (10-15 gal.) barrel or tub | Cool nights produce better quality fruit. Prune to keep shape. |
| Bean, String (*Phaseolus vulgaris*) (W) | Blue Lake, Kentucky Wonder, Greencrop, Poamoho, Mānoa Wonder, Hawaiian Wonder | 8-10 plants in 16" dia. barrel or tub | Train on trellis. Do not overwater. Watering leaves can spread disease. Harvest beans while young; pick regularly to keep plants producing. |
| Carrot (*Daucus carota*) (C) | Short N' Sweet, Lady Finger, Little Finger | veranda box at least 12" deep | Needs rich, cinder-free potting mix. Keep evenly moist. Do not overwater. Harvest before carrots become woody. |
| Chard (*Beta vulgaris* var. *cicla*) (C) | Bright Lights | 10" dia. pot | Cut colorful young leaves for salads. Will grow in part shade. |
| Cucumber (*Cucumis*) (W) | Spacemaster; spiny, climbing Asian types | 2 plants in 14" dia. pot | Train vines on trellis. Monitor closely for insects. Fine-mesh crop cover can be used to protect fruits, but hand-pollinating may be neccessary since cucumbers depend on insects for pollination. |
| Eggplant (*Solanum melongena*) (W) | Long types: Ichiban, Waimānalo Long. Round types: Black Beauty, Florida Market. Small types: Black Egg, Money Maker | 12" dia. pot | Harvest fruits before full size to encourage more fruits to grow. |
| Kumquat (*Fortunella crassifolia*) | Meiwa (round), Nagami (oval) | 16"-18" dia. tub or barrel (5-15 gal.) | Very attractive small tree in a small garden setting. Fruits are bright orange and bear annually, with fragrant blossoms. |
| Lettuce (*Lactuca sativa*) (C) | Cool weather: Anuenue, Mānoa (Green Mignonette), Bibb, Buttercrunch, Parris Island Cos Red Sails. Space-savers: Little Gem, Tom Thumb. Heat tolerant: Black Seeded Simpson Elite | Window box or grow as a companion to tomato in a tub or barrel | Keep cool and prevent bolting with some shade. Heat tolerant types are slow to bolt in summer. Protect from snails and slugs. |

## Vegetables & Fruits for Hawai'i Container Gardens

### W= Warm weather, C= Cool weather

| | | | |
|---|---|---|---|
| Onion, Green (*Allium fistulosum*) (W) | Multiplying types; Koba Strain is rust resistant. | window box | Buy small leaved types from grocer and plant stems. Large leaved types are grown from seed. |
| Peas, Snow/Sugar (*Pisum sativum*) (C) | Mānoa Sugar (powdery mildew resistant), Oregon Sugar, Dwarf Grey Sugar | 16" dia. tub or barrel | Use netting to protect from birds. Pick pods before seeds become large. |
| Pepper, Bell (*Capsicum annuum*) (C) | California Wonder, Yolo Wonder | 10-12" dia. pot | Less fruit when planted in summer. Better planted in late fall, winter. Harvest late winter, early spring. |
| Pepper, Hot (*Capsicum annuum*) (W) | Any type. Jalapeno and Hawaiian Chili do well. | 10" dia. pot | Small red chilis are attractive to birds. |
| Pineapple (*Ananas comosus*) (W) | Any tasty one you have eaten | 12" dia. pot | Save crown and plant in rich potting mix. Flowers during cool weather in December. Harvest 6 to 8 months later, in summer. |
| Radish (*Raphanus sativus*) (C) | Cherry Belle, French Breakfast, Scarlet Globe | window box | Plant in cool weather. |
| Spinach, Asian types (W) | Malabar *(Basella alba)*; Okinawan *(Gynura bicolor)* | 14" dia. pot | Not true spinaches, but tropical plants with lush growth and edible leaves. Okinawan spinach is tasty when fresh, a bit slimy when cooked. |
| Taro, Kalo (*Colocasia esculenta*) (W) | Many Hawaiian types; Chinese Bun Long leaves favored for laulau; Japanese *dasheen* or *araimo.* | 12-16" dia. pot, 8-10" deep | Plant 6-10" deep in center of pot. Double-potting with moist sphagnum moss raises humidity to good level. Also see Chapter 9 for more about Taro (Kalo). |
| Tomato *(Solanum lycopersicum)* (W) | Cherry types: Sweet 100, Sweet Million, Yellow Pear, Sun Gold. Patio types: Patio, Pixie Hybrid, Healani, Tiny Tim. Roma type: Roma, Juliet. | 16" dia. or larger tub or barrel | Train to cage, stake, or trellis. Can prune to three strong main vines. Smaller, thick-skinned types resist fruit flies better. Calcium produces more fruit. Avoid watering leaves. Pick fruit when 3/4 ripe. Cracking or splitting is due to heavy rainfall. |
| Squash, Summer *(Cucurbita pepo)* (W) | Zucchini, Summer Crookneck, Early Straightneck, White Scallop, Cocozelle | 16" dia. or larger tub or barrel | Monitor closely for insects. Bag fruit to protect from melon fly. Fine-mesh crop cover can be used to protect fruits, but hand-pollinating may be neccessary since squashes depend on bees for pollination. |

## EDIBLE FLOWERS

Grow edible flowers organically and add them sparingly to your salad for color and flavor. Use flowers pinched from basil and garlic chives. Nasturtiums are favored for their peppery, slightly sweet blossoms and young leaves. Try space-saving Cherry Rose, a variety of nasturtium that grows only 2 feet high and has a bushy habit.

## EASY BAMBOO TRELLIS

### Materials

- 3 bamboo stakes, 1-inch diameter, 6 to 8 feet long
- 1 zip cable tie
- Jute or other garden twine
- optional: square 8-inch concrete blocks, cinder or rocks for filler

### Instructions

1. If you have enough soil, dig 8-inch holes for the feet of the trellis. Or, for no-dig support, set each stake into a concrete block. Fill the blocks with rocks or cinder for extra stability after you put the trellis feet in place. Paint the concrete blocks if you like.

2. To bind the stakes together at the top, first make a loop with the cable tie by sliding one end through the other. (If it's threaded correctly it makes a zipping sound.) Hold one end of the stakes so that they are even and form a triangle when the tips are viewed head on. Position the cable tie below the first nodes of the bamboo, and then pull the cable tie tight.

3. Stand the trellis upright, and open it into a tripod. Position it over the container, and anchor the feet in the ground or in concrete blocks and cinder or gravel if needed, especially in windy areas.

4. Make the webbing for the trellis with twine. Start by tying the twine to the top of the trellis. Wind the twine downward in a spiral around the stakes. Tie the twine securely to each stake as you go along. After this is complete, weave the cross strings. Beginning at the top of the trellis, weave twine downward in each space between two stakes. Tie the twine where it crosses, so it looks something like a volleyball net. Do this for the remaining spaces.

As the plant grows, train the plant to the twine. You can make a bigger trellis by using more stakes or taller ones. Some people like to use stainless steel or copper wire instead of the plastic cable tie. Bamboo will eventually rot if put into the ground,

Trellises save space and improve air circulation, which helps prevent fungal diseases. This simple trellis is easy to make and use, take down and store. Bamboo is weather resistant, sturdy, inexpensive, and available from garden shops or even free from someone's backyard.

Baby Asian greens grow fast in a window box. Use a stick-on barrier of copper tape to keep snails and slugs away. Some gardeners swear by their own homemade slug repellents: crushed eggshells, coffee grounds, saucers of beer, or handpicking.

but you can always cut off the ends or reuse the stakes singly.

## BABY ASIAN GREENS WINDOW BOX

Growing greens has quick rewards, and you don't need as much sun to grow a successful harvest. Ensure a steady supply of greens by planting boxes at one-week intervals. Plastic window boxes hold moisture better than wood or clay, but keep them elevated off hot concrete surfaces. Placing containers off the ground also makes plants less accessible to slugs. Greens are more tender and milder in taste with some afternoon shade.

Some seed companies offer their own mixes of Asian greens, but you can make your own mix or plant a box with just one kind. Try *mizuna, won bok,* or mustard greens. You can keep snails and slugs from munching on your new seedlings by sticking on a barrier of a copper tape, available from some garden shops, around the sides of the window box. Scientific studies show snails and slugs won't cross copper tape because their slime interacts with it and causes an electrical charge that deters them.

Fill the box with potting mix, within 1 inch of the top. Incorporate a slow-release fertilizer. Plant the seeds as directed on the packet. Use a watering can to gently sprinkle water over the surface so that seeds remain in place. Water until the window box drains from the bottom.

Keep the window box evenly moist by watering at least once or twice a day. Watering in early morning and evening is best. Asian greens are best for salad and stir-fry when still young. Harvest them by snipping off the leaves with kitchen shears.

## CULINARY HERB GARDEN

Fresh herbs growing outside your kitchen are a cheery sight, and they save you money. Culinary herbs can be costly in the grocery store, and usually you end up with more than you need. Most herbs do well in 7- to 10-inch clay pots, but if you live in a hot, dry area, try planting them in terra-cotta-colored plastic pots, and then slipping the plastic pots into clay pots to achieve a more natural appearance. Give herbs water at least once a day in hot weather. For more flavorful herbs, use no fertilizer.

I like to grow each herb in its own pot so that I can provide the right amount of water. But you can also plant combinations of herbs that have the same water needs in the same container. It's fun to plant them together according to a culinary theme.

Rosemary (*Rosmarinus officinalis*) is easy to grow as topiary with a purchased wire frame.

Grow herbs that you actually like to use. This garden offers basil (*Ocimum basilicum*), rosemary (*Rosmarinus officinalis*), Berggarten sage (*Salvia officinalis* 'Berggarten'), lemon balm (*Melissa officinalis*), chives (*Allium shoenoprasum*) Asian garlic chives (*Allium tuberosum*), and red-flowering thyme (*Thymus serpyllum*).

Basil does best if kept in its own pot with moderate watering. Avoid overwatering, which can cause root rot. Pinch the tips of basil to keep it small and bushy—never let it flower, or it will get tall and leggy. I like to make pesto, but instead of growing one large plant I like to have an eye-appealing sampler's collection of several different kinds of basil and keep them small. During summer, I pinch the tips regularly and can keep the harvest for a short time in a plastic bag in the refrigerator. A half dozen or more 7-inch pots of assorted basil yield enough pinched tips to make a cup of pesto each week.

(above): Growing several small pots of basil (*Ocimum basilicum*) ensures a steady fresh supply. Back row: 'Purple Ruffles', 'African Blue'. Front row: "mystery basil" from a friend, 'Cuban', and 'Spicy Globe'.

(below): An herb garden of Thai basil (*Ocimum basilicum*), young galangal (*Alpinia galanga*), and lemongrass (*Cymbopogon citratus*).

## ASIAN HERB GARDEN

There are herbs used in Asian cooking that don't need much room to grow and are ornamental, too. If you want to learn more about the exotic herbs grown in Hawai'i, an excellent book to read is *Ethnic Culinary Herbs: A Guide to Identification and Cultivation in Hawai'i*, by George Staples and Michael S. Kristiansen (University of Hawai'i Press 1999). The authors tell you how to grow and use more than thirty herbs, including the ones listed here. Each of these herbs is best planted in its own container.

You can keep a Mexican herb garden for fresh-tasting tacos and salsas. Plant green onions (*Allium fistulosum*), cilantro (*Coriandrum sativum*), and oregano (*Origanum*) together in a Mexican clay pot. Pair it with another Mexican clay pot planted with a hot chile pepper such as Jalapeño or Habañero.

**Thai basil** (*Ocimum basilicum*). This is the nearly intoxicating, slightly licorice-scented basil you get in Vietnamese *pho* soup. In Thai cooking, the leaves are used in stir-fry dishes and seeds are used in desserts. Young leaves and flowers have a hint of purple. Maintain the same as other kinds of basil in full sun or indirect sun. Provide moderate water, pinch tips and flowers to encourage the plant to put out new side growth and become bushy.

**Lemongrass** (*Cymbopogon citratus*). Cultivated in India, Southeast Asia, Malaysia, and Singapore, lemongrass is 2 to 3 feet tall and has pale green leaves, which are used fresh or dried for tea. The most fragrant parts of the plant are the woody stalks, which are cut and crushed to release their flavor for curries, soups, and stews. Provide ample water and

with roots. Harvest only what you need and it will keep producing. You needn't pull up the whole plant.

**Water Mint** (*Mentha aquatica*). Water mint grows as a native in wet areas near streams and ponds in Europe and western Asia. It is a stronger flavored mint than the ones usually encountered in Western cooking. You need only a sprig of mint

(below): *Shiso* leaves (*Perilla frutescens*) are used for tofu dishes, sashimi, tempura, salads, and garnishes. The purple variety is used to color Japanese *umeboshi* (pickled plum) and young ginger.

(left): *Rau ram.*

full sun, and regularly remove dead leaves. Lemongrass needs good drainage. Use a large pot, and divide and repot clumps every 2 to 3 years.

***Rau Ram,*** or Vietnamese coriander (*Polygonum odoratum*). *Rau ram* is cultivated in Southeast Asia. Eat whole sprigs with spring rolls, or chop fresh leaves to serve with mint in salads. You can use it in place of cilantro in other dishes, though the taste is slightly different. I sometimes use *rau ram* leaves finely chopped in salsa and guacamole. *Rau ram* is a tropical plant, so it tolerates heat better than true coriander, which tends to bolt in hot weather. Plant it in rich organic potting mix, place in full or partial shade and provide ample water. Growing *rau ram* in containers is wise because it tends to creep and spread quickly in the garden. Trim it and use it to keep it compact.

**Green Onion** (*Allium fistulosum*). A must-have in Island kitchens, green onions are perhaps one of the easiest edibles to grow. Just grab a bunch in the grocery store, cut off the green tops, and plant the stalks

*Pandan (Pandanus amaryllifolius)* in a rustic clay pot from Vietnam.

with 3 sets of leaves to start a pot. You could even save a piece when you dine out. When you get home, stick the sprig into a pot with potting mix and keep it moist. Soon you'll have a pot full of green with invigorating fragrance, and you'll be glad you planted it in a container. Mint has a tendency to grow rapidly and can take over your entire garden. Mint is great to have on hand for refreshing iced drinks and to eat with spring rolls.

***Shiso*** (*Perilla frutescens*). Fragrant purple or green shiso is used in Japanese and Vietnamese dishes. Keep it in full sun to partial shade and provide ample water. *Shiso* grows tall quickly, so pinch off flowers to produce a shorter, fuller plant. At the end of a year, allow the plant to flower and mature with seeds so that you can replant.

***Pandan, pandan wangi*** (*Pandanus amaryllifolius*). Not the familiar hala tree of Hawai'i, but a cousin to it. Also known as dwarf screw pine. One whiff of the leaves and you'll think you're in a Thai restaurant—think of the heady scent of Jasmine rice. *Pandan* is used in Thai and Vietnamese cooking to make rice and sweets. It is also used to make scented water for religious ceremonies. Leaves can be dried or used fresh. Usually they are tied into a knot before being tossed into a pot of boiling liquid. *Pandan* needs full sun or partial shade and regular water. If given good drainage, it is an exquisite low-maintenance plant to keep on the lanai.

## GROW A POT OF EDIBLE GINGER

### Edible Ginger, 'Awapuhi Pākē (*Zingiber officinale*)

You can go to the grocery store and buy a piece of ordinary, commercially grown culinary ginger root and whip up some delectable Island cuisine, but growing your own ginger is more intriguing and rewarding. Ginger root isn't actually a root but is a rhizome, a thickened piece of the stem that is a storage organ for the plant. Young ginger is an Asian gourmet item that some folks love to eat pickled, and it is sometimes difficult to find unless you are lucky enough to have an Asian market in your area. You can grow your own young ginger, but remember that it does take a lot of young ginger to make pickles. Container growing avoids some of the problems caused by pests and diseases that may attack these plants, and a single pot of ginger at least assures you that you will have your own fresh, pungent supply growing close at hand.

(above): Young ginger sprouting in potting mix. Hilling, (adding more potting mix to the pot to cover the rhizomes,) allows growth to continue so that you can harvest more gingerroot.

In an attempt to find a way to reduce ginger wilt, a bacterial disease that has affected ginger farms in Hawai'i, the USDA and the University of Hawai'i College of Tropical Agriculture at Mānoa researched the advantages of ginger grown in containers under greenhouse conditions. In an experiment led by USDA scientist Dr. Francis Zee, each piece of wilt-free ginger-seed rhizome was planted in its own 15 gallon grow-bag that was filled with a soilless potting mix. After a program of watering, fertilizing, and hilling, the results were amazing: At harvest time each bag had an average yield of almost 15 pounds of rhizomes grown from a single 1-ounce ginger-seed piece! You probably wouldn't want that much ginger even for a year of nightly stir-frys. However, a 5-gallon pot of culinary ginger growing on your patio or lanai provides attractive greenery and an interesting conversation starter for dinner.

In a USDA experiment, a single grow-bag of soilless media produced a 26-pound ginger rhizome!

## How to Grow

The best time to start ginger is in March or April. Find a fresh, clean piece of edible ginger from the grocery store. Buy organic

(left): Young ginger can be harvested spring through summer. If you wait until late fall and early winter, the ginger plant matures and flowers. By January, you could have some fresh ginger ready for New Year celebrations.

Tomatoes for salads and lomilomi salmon, and "look ma, no weeding!" This upside-down cherry tomato was hanging in full sun under a clear polycarbonate roof. You can hang a bucket from other strong, stable support, as long as it's protected from heavy rainfall.

ginger from the natural food store, if you plan to go the organic route. Look for plump rhizomes (avoid any pieces that look shriveled or moldy or brown inside.) When you get home, cut the ginger into 1- to 2-ounce pieces. One piece will grow one plant. Each piece should have 2 to 4 well-developed "eyes." Let the cut ginger cure in a cool, dry place for about three days before planting.

Fill a 5-gallon pot with potting mix. You can fill it to one-third from the bottom if you want to try hilling your ginger to increase the yield. Plant the seed piece 2 inches deep in the potting mix. Fertilize using a balanced slow-release fertilizer according to manufacturer's directions. Place the pot in full sun. Keep the potting mix evenly moist through the year.

As the shoots grow, they push upward out of the potting mix. After about 3 months you will see the rhizomes growing out of the surface of the potting mix. At this point you can add more potting mix to cover them. This is called hilling, and it is practiced in the commercial production of ginger to accommodate the expanding growth of the ginger rhizomes. You may harvest young ginger in about 5 months. After 10 months or so, about December, the ginger plant matures and flowers. Stop watering, and allow the plant to naturally die and dry out.

After 3 weeks, cut off the wilted or wilting tops. Continue to keep the container dry for 3 more weeks. Then the mature gingerroot is ready to be removed from the container. Loosen the potting mix from the rhizomes. Cure in a clean, dry area. Wash only before use. Enjoy and share with friends, and remember to save a piece for replanting.

## HULI! UPSIDE-DOWN TOMATOES

It may look like a wacky science project, but growing tomatoes upside down has a practical rationale. Tomatoes grown in containers with a soilless potting mix have practically zero chance of developing root knot nematode and soil-borne diseases, and plants stay out of reach of slugs and snails. Amaze your friends and amuse your family! You may have the honor of being the most envied tomato magician on your block as tomatoes tumble from the sky, ripe and juicy for salads and sauces.

Growing upside-down tomatoes is great fun for you, but of course this is totally unnatural for the plant. There are a few drawbacks. Water that has leached fertilizer can drip from the hole onto the leaves. Wet leaves in hot, humid weather can lead to powdery mildew. As the tomato plant grows, the branches must be tied up to keep them from snapping off or touching the ground. A 5-gallon bucket filled with potting mix is heavy, even heavier when watered and bearing fruits. The 5-gallon size accommodates the mature tomato plant's roots better so that it will bear more fruit, but if this size is too heavy you can try planting in a 3-gallon container.

Choose tomato varieties with medium or small fruit, such as Roma or cherry tomatoes. Large-fruited ones will be too heavy and will have branches that break; these types are also more prone to calcium deficiency. You can also try growing peppers and eggplants.

## Materials

- Organic potting mix
- Fertilizer, compost
- 5-gallon bucket
- Newspaper or sphagnum moss
- Tomato plant in a 4-inch pot

## Instructions

Prepare the potting mix. You can use a synthetic slow-release fertilizer such as Osmocote or Nutricote, or try an organic granular fertilizer. Follow manufacturer's directions. Five gallons of potting mix is heavy even before watering, so you may want to make the mix lighter by blending in more perlite. Be sure the potting mix is moist and not sludgy.

Cut a 2½-inch hole in the bottom of the bucket. Place the bucket atop a work surface that will allow the top of the plant to dangle freely from the hole on the bottom. Straddle it between two tables, a couple of sawhorses, or other stable surfaces that will safely support it.

Line the hole with something to hold the tomato plant in place until it grows enough root structure to hold in the potting mix. Moistened sphagnum moss looks nice, but you can use plain newspaper. An easy way to use newspaper is to take half of a page, fold it into fourths, cut an 'X' and fold the flaps open wide enough to accommodate the leaves of the tomato plant when you pass them through.

A) Cut a 2 ½-inch hole in the botton of a 5-gallon bucket. Line the hole with newspaper or sphagnum moss. Place the bucket on a surface with a space where the tomato plant will be able to hang freely without getting crushed.

B) Add enough potting mix so that the roots will be at the correct depth when upside down. Leave the opening clear so that it will be easy to pass the plant through the hole.

C) Carefully insert the plant through the hole. You can bundle the leaves together with a plastic bag to make it easier to pass them through the hole. Adjust the planting depth if necessary.

D) Add more potting mix until the level reaches within 3 inches from the top of the bucket. Then hang the bucket from a strong support in full sun, and water the plant through the top of the bucket. You can suspend the bucket by a strong chain from the eaves of the house so that it has enough exposure to sun and is not shaded by the roof. A sturdy clothesline pole also works. Don't let the bucket fill up with rain—cover it with a lid to prevent it from becoming soggy and too heavy.

Gently pass the plant through the hole, leaves first. You can wrap the leaves in a plastic bag or a sheet of moist newspaper to make it easier to pass the top of the plant through the hole. Mound the potting mix around the stem of the tomato to the desired planting depth. (Think in reverse. If you were planting the tomato right-side-up, you would plant the stem deeper than it was in the original pot to encourage a stronger root system to grow.)

Everbearing strawberries (*Fragaria* hybrid) 'Berri Basket' in a hanging wire basket lined with sphagnum moss.

Continue adding potting mix until it reaches about 3 inches below the top of the bucket.

When watered, the bucket can weigh about 50 pounds! You can hang the bucket from a chain fastened to a strong support such as the eaves of your house or a clothesline pole, as long as the plant will get full sun. Add water through the top of the bucket when the potting mix is dry on the surface. Protect the bucket from becoming soggy and heavy during rainy periods with a lid or plastic bag.

## HANGING STRAWBERRY BASKET

Imagine sitting on your lanai at breakfast and being able to reach up to grab a handful of ripe, juicy strawberries for your cereal bowl. Yum! A hanging wire basket lined with sphagnum moss and planted with strawberries is a welcome sight on your patio in the morning. You can line a wire basket yourself, or for convenience use one that is pre-lined with dry compressed moss that you fluff up with just a spritz of water. Fill the moistened basket with rich organic potting mix. A 14-inch basket will hold three or four 4-inch transplants. As they grow, they will send out runners that you can tuck into the moss on the sides of the basket. Make a hole in the moss in the side and insert the roots of a runner into the potting mix. You can do this for a few evenly spaced runners, but you should cut off the rest. You don't want to overload the capacity of the potting mix to sustain the plants. As the plants fill out, the basket will grow into a "ball" of green with its sweet bounty. Although you'll have no problems with snails or slugs, it may be necessary to protect your basket with netting to prevent birds from getting to your fruit.

Strawberries are heavy feeders so fertilize regularly with a liquid fertilizer in addition to a slow-release one. Water the basket inside and out at least once daily, twice if neccessary.

Keep the moss and the potting mix moist and do not let them dry out.

Another way to maximize the outside planting area of the basket is to grow lettuce. Fill about a third of the basket with potting mix. Poke holes in the sides and insert four small looseleaf lettuce transplants such as Mānoa or Buttercrunch. Fill the rest of the basket with potting mix, and plant the strawberries. You'll have a harvest of lettuce for sandwiches and salads while you're waiting for the strawberries to ripen.

## KRATKY'S HANG-LOOSE HYDROPONIC LETTUCE

It's the ultimate laid-back gardener's dream. After about 10 minutes of set up, there's no additional watering, fertilizing or weeding. Just kick back and wait 5 to 6 weeks, and you'll be able to harvest fresh homegrown lettuce on your lanai or porch. This super-simple method for growing lettuce hydroponically in a small container was developed by UH researcher Dr. Bernard Kratky, who also owns the patent. You may use his method to grow at home or for educational purposes, but there are specific restrictions regarding commercial uses that require Dr. Kratky's permission.*

### Materials

- 1 gallon plastic cranberry juice bottle or equivalent with 1½-inch opening
- 1 teaspoon of hydroponic fertilizer

Growing hydroponic lettuce can be a science project full of discovery for youngsters. A gallon milk jug can be cut to fit a net pot for a simple noncirculating system. Photo: Glenn Sako

Purchase net pots like these, 3 inches long and 1 ½ inches in diameter, or make your own from plastic cups.

After making the nutrient solution, fill the net pot with growing medium. Tap it so it settles, and do not compact it.

Growing medium should become moist through capillary action. Or you can add 1 to 2 tablespoons of water to moisten before planting seeds.

Plant one or two seeds 1/4-inch deep in the growing medium. Cover lightly with the medium. Cover the bottle if it is not opaque to prevent algae growth.

(Chem-Gro 10-8-22 or equivalent)
- 1 net pot (1½-inch diameter x 3 inches long)
- Growing medium (may contain at least two of the following: peat, perlite, vermiculite, coir)
- Lettuce or *kai choy* seeds

Purchase net pots from a hydroponic supply company or garden shop. As a substitute you can use a similar-sized plastic cup with holes. Use seed before its expiration date and be sure that it has been properly stored in a cool, dry place. Keep unused seed in the refrigerator. Heat-tolerant varieties such as Black Seeded Simpson Elite perform best.

Dr. Kratky said that in order for the method to work, the pots must be able to:
- Contain the growing medium
- Be long enough to be submerged when first planted
- Have enough holes for the roots to grow through to reach down into the bottle

## Instructions for Kratky's Method

- Rinse the plastic bottle with water a few times to remove any residues.
- Add a teaspoon of hydroponic fertilizer to the bottle.
- Make the nutrient solution by adding about 1 quart of water to the bottle and swirl it to dissolve some of the fertilizer. The water will turn cloudy, and some fertilizer will come to rest at the bottom.
- Fill the bottle with water to about 1 ½ inches from the top.
- Fill the net pot with growing medium. Tap it so the medium settles. Do not pack.
- Put the net pot with the medium into the top of the bottle. It should fit without any gaps, otherwise your setup could become a haven for breeding mosquitoes. The bottom half of the net pot should sit in the nutrient solution.
- The growing medium should wick up the solution and become moist. If it is still dry

A large noncirculating hydroponic system needs a greenhouse or similar outdoor structure with clear plastic sheeting or roofing to allow adequate sunlight and to provide protection from rain. In this backyard greenhouse in Hilo, a growing table lined with black plastic and covered with foam sheets was used to grow Red Butterhead and Red Romaine lettuce varieties. For advice on how to build your own system, call the Hawai'i County Extension Office. Photo: Glenn Sako.

at the top, carefully add a teaspoon or two of water to the medium in the pot.

- Make a ¼-inch hole in the growing medium, and plant 1 or 2 seeds. Cover the seeds lightly with medium.

Place your bottle on a patio, lanai, porch, or under the overhang of the house. It should be protected from rain and wind and still receive bright, indirect sunlight. To prevent the nutrient solution from growing algae that can slow the growth of your lettuce, block out the light. Paint the bottle, put a paper grocery sack around it, or wrap it with aluminum foil.

For the next 5 to 6 weeks, relax. No peeking! Don't pull the net pot from the bottle or you will damage the roots. You don't need to add any more water or fertilizer. In fact, if more water is added, you will probably cause damage to the plant.

After you harvest the lettuce, pull out the remaining roots and medium from the net pot. Rinse out the net pot and the bottle to reuse.

## Stick Your Head in an Ice Bucket

Master gardener Elaine Munro of Pepe'ekeo adapted Kratky's method to grow two heads of lettuce in a Styrofoam ice bucket. For this setup she used 4-inch net pots.

Using a drywall drill bit slightly smaller than the net pots, she drilled two holes in the lid of an ice bucket. Elaine discovered the lid seated better if it was placed upside down over the bucket.

She lined the ice bucket with a black plastic bag and trimmed the excess. Two gallons of nutrient solution filled the ice bucket.

Into each net pot she put damp sphagnum moss, making it three-quarters full. Then she placed a moist grow-cube of peat on top of the moss. She planted her lettuce seeds into the cubes. Damp vermiculite filled in the rest of the spaces in the net pots. Each pot fit snugly into a drilled hole.

Elaine recommended that you make sure the bottom of the net pot will reach the nutrient solution. If it doesn't, you should use a wick, such as a piece of cotton rope or terry cloth strip. The ice bucket excludes light, so it doesn't grow algae. Elaine tied the lid down with string so that curious guests wouldn't inadvertently disturb her mysteriously successful operation.

If you plant five or six buckets or bottles at one-week intervals, you can harvest lettuce each week. Invite family and friends to sample your greens, and tell them the fascinating story about how your lettuce came from a bottle. Or you can keep the secret to yourself and instead impress them with a yarn about the many long, sweaty hours you worked in the garden just to serve them an 'ono homegrown salad.

*Notice: This hydroponic method is protected by U.S. Patents 5,385,589 and 5,533,299. The method may be used freely in Hawai'i for hobby and educational purposes. In addition, commercial farmers are free to grow crops with this technology in Hawai'i. However, permission must be granted from UH researcher Dr. Bernard Kratky for the commercial manufacturing and sale of hydroponic kits utilizing this technology and for selling or licensing this technology within the State of Hawai'i, plus these and any commercial uses beyond the State of Hawai'i.

One Styrofoam ice bucket can grow two heads of hydroponic lettuce at once.

# 7 Unusual & Thrifty Containers

On the plantation, concrete pots were made by hand using molds such as these.

## PLANTATION COLLECTIBLES

On your next Island hop, look for planting containers in antique and collectible stores and get a peek into the local history. During the plantation days, objects that could not be bought had to be crafted by hand, including copper buckets and concrete flowerpots. Old-time wooden tubs that once held *shoyu*, *sake*, or rice make unique containers for plants. Vintage ceramic bonsai pots imported to Hawaiʻi generations ago make elegant dish gardens. They also make gorgeous presentations of freeform dwarf bamboo, succulents, potted palms, and orchids.

(right): *Carludovica* in an antique handmade copper bucket.

(below): Succulent String-of-Pearls (*Senecio rowleyanus*) seems to bubble over this reused tea kettle.

## FLEA MARKET FUN

Former plant nursery manager Betty Baker was fascinated with plants for decades, ever since she was a teenager and she received a mother-in-law's tongue plant as a gift. People who met her at the farmer's market in Puna on the Big Island knew her skill with plants and would bring her anything that could hold even a tiny bit of potting mix—old cooking pots, toys, plastic spray can tops, shoes, and collectible ceramic doodads—in which she planted succulents and cacti, some of them rare.

Lady palm (*Rhapis excelsa*) in a vintage bonsai pot marks a partially shaded entryway.

A discarded toy gets new life with a tiny load of potting mix and succulent *Haworthia*.

A recycled plastic colander has plenty of drainage holes for this unusual succulent (*Erythrorhipsalis*).

(far left): Look out, she's one sharp tūtū.

(left): Playful dish gardens of succulents in cast-off kitchenware and a thrift-shop ceramic kewpie.

When she received a recyclable container, she didn't plant in it immediately. She waited for one of her plants to tell her that it should be planted in it, and the rest is whimsical history.

## RE-TIRED IN HAWAI'I

When grocery store owner Hiroshi Akamine decided it was time to retire from the business, he didn't give up his vegetables entirely. He wanted to have a vegetable garden in his golden years, so he began digging in the soil of his home in Hilo. However, it was so full of rocks it seemed useless to continue. So he took a different approach. He filled the area for the garden with a layer of well-draining blue rock gravel. Then he used a sharp knife to cut off the rims of old rubber tires—back when he was a strong *young* retired man, he says—and he stacked them atop the gravel. He filled the tire stacks with soil trucked in from Pepe'ekeo, added chicken manure, and then he planted his favorite fruits and veggies.

Hiroshi stayed healthy with the exercise he got by working in his garden and eating his own fresh, homegrown vegetables. In his recycled tire container garden he grew soybeans, pineapples, papayas, green onions, string beans, lettuce, eggplant, bittermelon, ginger, chives, *daikon,* and sweet potatoes. He replanted with the seeds he saved from each harvest. After 25 years the retired-but-still-working tire garden still had no sign of

Even pineapple and papaya get good mileage in this tire garden.

Green onions and soybeans grow in recycled rubber tires that left the road a quarter of a century ago.

An old coconut was sliced at the top for planting and at the bottom for drainage, and then filled with potting mix to make a unique vessel for a dracaena.

giving up, and neither did Hiroshi. In 2006, Hiroshi celebrated his 90th birthday with a trip to Las Vegas.

## COCONUT ORCHID PLANTER

In Thailand, orchids grow out of coconuts. Hawai'i restaurant owner Padina T. Wu grew orchids outside her establishment the way she remembered they do back in Thailand. She found a whole old, dry coconut ("The kind nobody wants," she said) and cut off the top to create an opening for the plant. The next step took a bit of doing. With a knife she partially pried the husk, carefully separating it into small sections as if making a many-petaled lotus. Next, she bent wire around the coconut husk to help keep its shape. Then she put an orchid plant straight into the coconut container with no other media added. Tina used inexpensive macramé plant hangers to suspend the containers from the roof beams outside her restaurant. Once in a while she added fertilizer, but other than that the orchids were carefree in coconut heaven, their roots growing right into the water-retaining coconut fiber.

Orchids love this cleverly handmade coconut planter.

(right): This unfinished wooden drum was completed with portulaca (*Portulaca grandiflora*).

(far right): Look for handmade artisan containers at craft fairs and nonprofit arts fund raisers. These pots were made by artists with disabilities for the Hawai'i Artists Cooperative.

(right): Although it looks made from newly cooled lava, this rough-textured lava pot imprinted with iridescent leaf patterns is made of concrete by artists Patti Datloff and Karen Hagen of Kea'au, Hawai'i.

(far right): Water garden in a large handcrafted composite clay and cement lava pot by artist Mark Kimball of Kailua-Kona, Hawai'i.

# 8 Maintenance

So you've made the investment in containers, plants, and potting mix. Now comes the commitment to keep everything healthy and growing. Care for your container plantings every day if possible, and monitor changes in plant health. Every location is different, and you are the true expert of that space where you place your containers. You can get great advice from books, the Internet, a friend, or an extension agent, but ultimately, you determine the finer points. Get to know the unique Hawaiian microclimate you live in by observing the subtle seasonal changes in your garden. Your personal experience is the best teacher.

### Common Mistakes in Container Gardening

- Too much fertilizer
- No fertilizer
- Too much water
- No water
- Not enough light
- Wrong location: poor circulation, too windy, etc.

## WATERING

When conditions are dry, plants in the ground have the opportunity to spread their roots over more area and to reach water stored deeper in the soil. However, plants

**Mōhala i ka wai ka maka o ka pua.**
Translation: "Unfolded by the water are the faces of the flowers." Flowers thrive where there is water, as thriving people are found where the living conditions are good.

—Ōlelo No'eau 2178

Choose a watering can that feels good in your hands. A 2-gallon can with a removable nozzle is a versatile choice.

in containers are dependent on whatever amount of water happens to fill up that small volume of potting mix in which they are confined, be it rain or the water you bestow upon them. Even if your plants are outside and exposed to rain, you still need to check on them everyday. Take note of changes in the weather. Did it rain last night? How much? Here in Hawai'i we are accustomed to overnight cooling showers, but they don't always provide enough water for a container plant that has to make it through a hot afternoon the next day. In the morning, check the surface of the potting mix. If the potting mix looks and feels dry, it needs water.

My own preference for watering container plantings is the good old-fashioned watering can. Unlike commercial plant growers who have many benches with the same kind of plant in the same kind of container, most home gardeners have a variety of plants with different requirements. Watering by hand saves water, and it allows you to adjust the amount of water you are giving to your plant according to its individual needs. Water a container until it drains from the bottom. While you're watering you can also inspect your plants for pests and take note of any necessary pinching and pruning. For outdoor watering, a versatile choice is a two-gallon watering can, a handy size for mixing liquid fertilizers. A wide opening for filling and a removable sprinkler head are other helpful features.

If you water with a garden hose that sits in the sun, the water might be hot when you first turn on the tap. Let the hot water run out first so that you don't cook your plants. The same goes for when you fill up watering cans with the hose, too.

Less intensive are automatic drip irrigation systems, which are convenient and save you time. Kits for patio and lanai are relatively inexpensive and come with directions for setup. These easily connect to an outside hose bib. They usually include microtubing, connectors, nozzles, plus fasteners to install your system. An automatic timer is usually sold separately and is the biggest expense. A battery-operated one eliminates the need for any electrical wiring. Automatic drip irrigation systems can water potted plants on the lanai and even hanging baskets. Try to place containers near each other so that it is easier to hide the microtubing and to conserve moisture. There are different nozzles to choose from that can deliver water in various ways, from a fine continuous mist to slow, regular droplets.

Water bromeliads from the top so that their cupped leaves can catch and hold water. Let bromies dry between waterings to avoid overwatering, which can lead to root rot. Flush them out occasionally to prevent build up of salts and mosquito larvae.

Most container plants need water every day, sometimes twice a day. It's best to water in the early morning and early evening. Avoid overhead watering in the middle of the day. The sun can magnify water droplets and cause leaves to burn. Also, some diseases spread more rapidly if plants are stressed and watered under the hot sun. Plants that

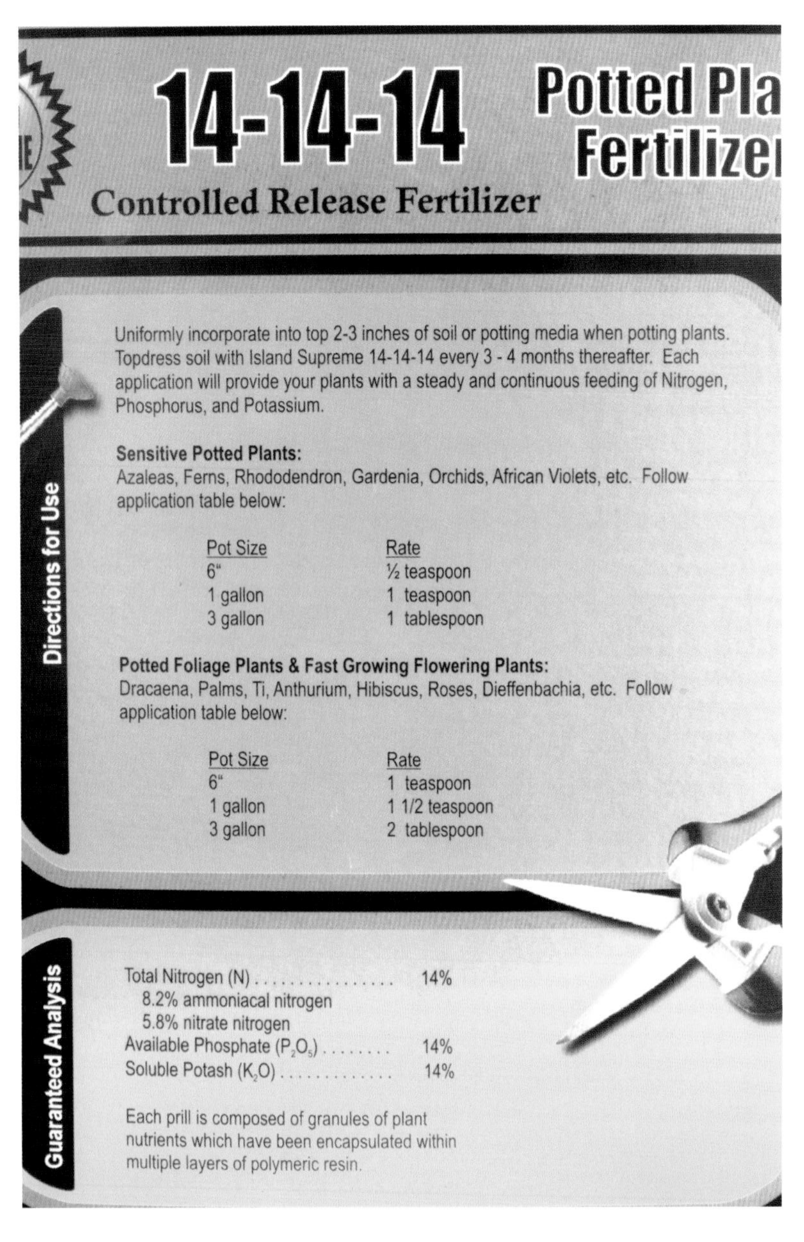


The guaranteed analysis is the amount of nitrogen (N), phosphorus (P), and potassium (K), plus micronutrients if they are included, by weight.

are less thirsty, such as succulents and cacti, need water only every two or three days. Too much water causes them to rot, so in times of constant heavy rain, move them to shelter.

Some gardeners swear by self-watering containers and won't use anything else. Self-watering containers can be useful especially if you go away for a few days, but they don't eliminate the need for watering. You still have to remember to check on your plants and top off the reservoir, and it might be easy to forget to do this if you're not a creature of habit. Most self-watering containers have a tendency to keep the media constantly wet. Some plants will do extremely well like this, but others might rot. If you get a container with a removable reservoir you at least have an option if things aren't working out.

## FERTILIZING

Container plantings are watered more frequently, and nutrients are leached out more quickly. It's important to regularly fertilize your container plants so that they continue to grow vigorously. But what exactly is fertilizer, and why do plants need it?

There are three major nutrients required by plants. Commercial fertilizers are labeled with a guaranteed analysis showing the amounts of these three major nutrients: nitrogen (N), phosphorus (P), and potassium (K). Each of the three numbers on the label corresponds to the amount of N-P-K in the fertilizer. That is, the first number is the amount of nitrogen, the second is phosphorus, and the third is potassium. When comparing fertilizers, think of these numbers as ratios. For example, a fertilizer that has an N-P-K of 3-1-2 delivers the same kind of nutrition as a fertilizer with an analysis of 24-8-16. The numbers represent the percentage of each element by weight. For example, a 50-pound bag of 14-14-14 contains 7 pounds of nitrogen, 7 pounds of phosphorus, and 7 pounds of potassium (50 x 0.14 = 7).

Nitrogen promotes more leafy growth, so a fertilizer with a higher amount of nitrogen such as 19-6-12 is good for plants being grown for their foliage. On the other hand, some fruiting plants need less nitrogen and higher levels of phosphorous and potassium or they won't produce fruit. A balanced fertilizer is one that has the same three numbers, such as 14-14-14. A balanced slow-release fertilizer is a good choice for growing most flowering plants.

Minors, or micronutrients, are also important for plants to flourish, but to a lesser degree. Some plants perform better

Synthetic slow-release fertilizers can last several months but break down faster with high temperature and humidity.

with more of a particular micronutrient. For example, tomatoes and culinary ginger are more productive with added calcium such as dolomite. Synthetic fertilizers list minors on the label if they are included. Organic fertilizers naturally contain minors, but the amounts can vary greatly.

Either synthetic or organic fertilizers can be used to provide the nutrition necessary to keep plants healthy. Slow-release fertilizers are less likely to burn and don't need to be applied as often. Organic fertilizers such as well-composted manures, bone meal, blood meal and so on are considered slow-release because they break down gradually. Synthetic slow-release fertilizers such as Osmocote or Nutricote are more expensive than synthetic granular fertilizers, but worth it in the long run for container gardening.

Some synthetic slow-release fertilizer manufacturers claim their products last for four months or more. This is true under certain conditions but in Hawai'i a number of factors, such as higher temperatures and frequent rain, can cause fertilizers to break down more quickly. A rainy, hot, humid environment can shorten the period between fertilizer applications and might last only three months. When using a fertilizer for the first time, follow the manufacturer's directions so that you don't overfertilize. Experience will tell you what adjustments to make.

## How to Fertilize

When planting, some gardeners prefer to place fertilizer on top of the potting mix (topdressing), and others like to mix it in. Either method works, but there is an advantage to topdressing when using synthetic slow-release fertilizers. Synthetic slow-release fertilizers are made up of many tiny individual beads. Each bead, or prill, has a coating specially formulated to dissolve slowly over time. Mixing the prills with cinder or other abrasive material can break the coating. Then you no longer have a slow-release fertilizer, but a quick-release fertilizer that can burn your plants. Or it will be used up quickly and not give you your money's worth. The beads gradually release their contents over time, but empty beads will still be visible. Keep track of your fertilizer schedule on a calendar, and remember to add a fresh supply every third month or so.

Liquid fertilizers give plants an extra boost quickly, providing them with nutrition in a form they can use almost immediately. This is an advantage when a plant is yellowing from a lack of adequate nutrition and needs help right away. Liquid fertilizer can be applied as a foliar spray or a drench to the potting mix. Some drawbacks of using liquid fertilizers exclusively are that they wash out of the container rapidly and, if not diluted properly, can burn the plant. Heavy feeders such as vegetables and fruits benefit greatly from a weekly supplemental dose of liquid fertilizer.

Fertilizer salts can build up in the potting mix, or on the outside surface of a clay pot over time. If the margins of the leaves begin to brown, salts could be the culprit. Gently tip the plant, shake off the media, and replant into a cleaned pot with new media. A clay pot should be soaked overnight and scrubbed with a brush. Resoak, sterilize if needed (see pg. 10), then reuse.

If a little fertilizer works wonders, more must be better, right? Not quite. It's better to err on the side of too little fertilizer than too much fertilizer. Overfertilizing with nitrogen, for instance, can result in lush green growth that seems to indicate health, but in fact is a sign of a stressed plant. Plants in this condition are irresistible to sucking and chewing insects that can further weaken the plant. Overfertilizing and poor watering methods can also result in stunting and leaves turning brown at the tips. If you live near a river, stream, or other waterway or area that empties into the ocean, remember that runoff from your gardening activities has an effect on those environments. Excessive fertilizer runoff can upset the balance of natural habitats, so use fertilizers wisely and sparingly.

## SYNTHETIC VERSUS ORGANIC FERTILIZERS

Should you use organic or synthetic fertilizers? I prefer organic fertilizers for my fruits and vegetables in containers and in the backyard because they break down slowly and are better for the environment. I've used synthetic slow-release fertilizers for houseplants and some ornamentals on the lanai. My edible plants get a weekly feeding of fish and seaweed fertilizers, and occasional doses of compost and earthworm castings to provide them with necessary

Left, liquid fish emulsion; right, seaweed extract as a soluable powder. When diluted with water, these organic fertilizers provide major nutrients and micronutrients in a form plants can take up quickly.

Pinching off flower spikes on coleus (*Coleus x hybridus*) prevents it from maturing and going to seed and helps keep it compact.

micronutrients. Some gardeners like to fertilize with homemade compost tea, which is also a good idea if you have the space, time, and inclination. There are two forms of compost tea. One is an easy anaerobic process that actually results in compost extract. Place a shovelful of compost into a burlap bag, tie it up, and suspend it from a tripod (like the one in Chapter 6). Let it steep for a week or two in a bucket of water. Use the compost extract as a drench or dilute it for foliar feeding. The second method is more involved and won't be covered here, but the good news is that it is aerobic and requires only 24 hours plus aeration equipment to brew a potent compost tea, which is full of beneficial microorganisms.

## PLUCKING, PINCHING, PRUNING, POTTING

Container plantings look their best with the regular upkeep of the four Ps.

**Plucking.** Pluck or snip off dead or yellowing leaves. Deadheading (removing old spent flowers from ornamentals) encourages more blooming and prevents the plant from going to seed. Harvest anything that's edible and has seeds before it becomes too mature so that the plant will keep producing.

**Pinching.** Some plants, such as coleus and basil, grow quickly, put out flowers, and then become tall and leggy. To extend the life of these types of plants, remove the tips where small flower buds are forming by pinching them off or snipping with pruners.

**Pruning.** Woody plants, such as citrus and pīkake, sometimes need shaping to keep them compact. Prune off scraggly branches and dead wood. Remove dry, old vines, and trim trailing plants that have become too long or sparse to bring back their lushness. In most cases, you can remove up to a third of a plant without harm.

**Potting.** Repotting, that is. Signs of a plant that has grown too large for the container and needs repotting include roots growing out of the drainage holes and small, yellowing leaves. Move up the plant to a container one size larger. Loosen the roots, or if necessary make a few spaced cuts with pruners or a sharp knife. If you want to try to keep the plant in the same pot, loosen and carefully prune the roots by a conservative amount—never trim more than 50 percent of the root ball. Repot with fresh potting mix.

(right): A mini-pressure sprayer is useful for applying foliar fertilizer and insecticidal soap.

(below): What to do with pruned-off potbound roots? This gardener made a wreath to hold *Tillandsia* air plants.

## PESTS

Gardeners newly arrived in Hawai'i are surprised to find that year-round gardening weather also means a year-round cycle of diseases and insects. With no cold winter to kill them, nonnative pests have found a paradise in Hawai'i, too. Fortunately, many problems caused by pests are preventable by keeping up with regular maintenance.

When plants become weak and stressed they are more susceptible to diseases and predation by insects. Choose plants that are more resistant to pests, and locate them in the best possible location. If pests do become a problem, don't reach for the deadliest, most potent pesticide available. Try to solve it with the solution that is least harmful to human health and the environment. If a plant develops disease or becomes a host for insects, isolate it immediately. Remove and dispose of the diseased parts. Handpick insects or spray with insecticidal soap. Remember that insecticides will also kill beneficial insects that predate on the insects you are trying to exterminate. Killing beneficial insects can actually contribute to creating a greater population of pests over time, so before spraying it's wise to wait first to see if biological controls can take care of the problem. Many gardeners report success with homemade remedies, and some are scientifically proven. However, some can be toxic. For an interesting discussion on homemade remedies, read *The Truth About Garden Remedies: What Works, What Doesn't, and Why* by Jeff Gillman (Timber Press 2006).

Hawai'i has many tropical pests that are unfamiliar to gardeners in North America. Your local extension office can help with identification and can suggest possible controls. Too many home gardeners mistakenly overuse pesticides. Read and follow the label. Remember, more is not better.

# 9 Plants for Hawai'i Container Gardens

## PALMS AND CYCADS

If you were to draw a cartoon of a desert island, what would it look like? Chances are you'd include a palm tree. The image of the palm is so firmly ingrained in our ideas of island vegetation that it's hard to imagine such a setting without at least one. Palms instantly infuse indoor and outdoor living spaces with a tropical atmosphere, and when trade winds blow the fronds make good garden music. Many palms adapt well in containers, often staying smaller than they would be if planted in the ground. In Hawai'i, most varieties of potted palms are easy to grow. Some palms prefer shade, and these do well indoors, under a protected porch or on a shady lanai. Those that prefer full sun are best on a sunny lanai or accenting an entryway.

Young palms need filtered sun until they toughen up and mature. Provide regular watering and a slow-release balanced fertilizer with micronutrients. Magnesium, zinc, and manganese are vital micronutrients for palms. They also respond well to fish emulsion. As a palm grows, let it nearly fill the pot but move it up to a larger pot before it becomes root-bound. Remove dead brown fronds to keep potted palms looking their best.

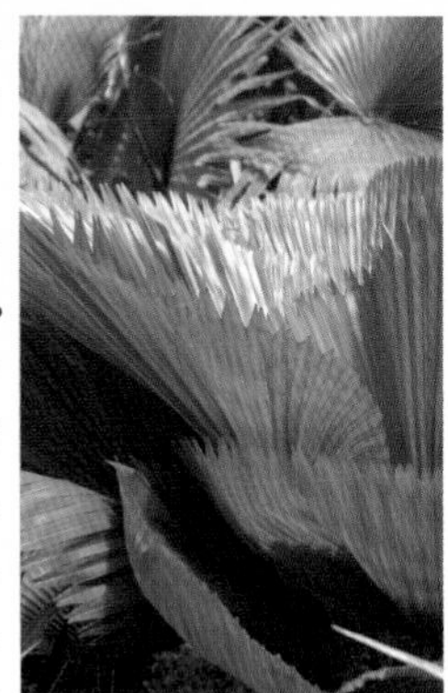

(above right): Licuala palm (*Licuala grandis*)

(left): Areca palm (*Dypsis lutescens*)

What about coconuts? If it gets full to part sun, a coconut palm looks great in a container, until it develops the first 4 or 5 fronds. After that, it has to be planted in the ground.

Cycads look like palms but they are actually prehistoric plants from the Mesozoic Era, the Age of Dinosaurs. They naturally blend well with tropical and Asian themes.

(above): Parlor palm (*Chamaedorea elegans*)

(right): The base of this palm is planted with trailing golden pothos (*Epipremnum pinnatum* 'Aureum').

## Palms for Containers

| COMMON NAME (*Botanical name*) | LIGHT REQUIREMENT | WATERING | NOTES |
|---|---|---|---|
| Areca (*Dypsis lutescens*) | Full sun, partial shade | High | Naturally golden yellow in full sun |
| Bamboo palm (*Chamaedorea seifrizii*) | Shade | High | No wind, can grow indoors |
| Black palm (*Normanbya normanbyi*) | Full sun | High | Moderate grower |
| Blue Hesper palm (*Brahea armata*) | Full sun | Low | Thorns, slow grower |
| Bottle palm (*Hyophorbe lagenicaulis*) | Full sun | Mod | Slow grower |
| Carpentaria palm (*Carpentaria acuminata*) | Full sun | High | Fast grower, not salt tolerant |
| Cascade palm (*Chamaedorea cataractarum*) | Partial shade | High | No harsh wind or salt, can grow indoors |
| Fishtail palm (*Caryota mitis*) | Full sun, partial shade | High | No salt tolerance, can grow indoors |
| Foxtail palm (*Wodyetia bifurcata*) | Full sun | Mod | Fast grower |
| Hardy Bamboo palm (*Chamaedorea microspadix*) | Shade | High | Protect from wind |
| Ivory Cane palm (*Pinanga kuhlii*) | Shade | High | Fast grower |
| Jamaican Thatch palm (*Thrinax parviflora*) | Full sun, light shade | Mod | Salt tolerant |
| Kentia palm (*Howea forsteriana*) | Part sun, part shade | Mod | Slow grower, can grow indoors |
| Lady palm (*Rhapis excelsa*) | Part sun to shade | High | Wind and salt tolerant, can grow indoors |
| Licuala palm (*Licuala grandis*) | Light shade | High | Thorns, protect from wind |
| Loulu palm (*Pritchardia hillebrandii*) | Full sun | High | Native palm, slow grower, salt tolerant |
| MacArthur palm (*Ptychosperma macarthurii*) | Light shade | High | Protect from wind |
| Manila palm (*Veitchia merrillii*) | Full sun, partial shade | High | Salt tolerant, can grow indoors |

| COMMON NAME (*Botanical name*) | LIGHT REQUIREMENT | WATERING | NOTES |
|---|---|---|---|
| Metallica (*Chamaedorea metallica*) | Shade | High | Protect from wind, no salt tolerance |
| Parlor palm (*Chamaedorea elegans*) | Shade | Mod | Protect from wind, can grow indoors |
| Princess palm (*Dictyosperma album*) | Light shade | High | Protect from wind |
| Sealing Wax palm (*Cyrtostachys renda*) | Full sun | High | Protect from wind |
| Shortstalked Chamaedorea (*Chamaedorea brachypoda*) | Shade | High | Can grow indoors |
| Silver palm (*Coccothrinax argentea*) | Full sun | Low | Salt and wind tolerant, can grow indoors |
| Thurston Fan palm (*Pritchardia thurstonii*) | Full sun | Mod | Slow grower, salt tolerant, can grow indoors |
| Triangle palm (*Dypsis decaryi*) | Full sun | Mod | Wind and heat tolerant |

Licuala Palm
*(Licuala ramsayi)*

## Cycads for Containers

| COMMON NAME (*Botanical name*) | LIGHT REQUIREMENT | WATERING | NOTES |
|---|---|---|---|
| Bamboo cycad (*Ceratozamia hildae*) | Partial shade | Mod | Easy to grow |
| Cardboard palm (*Zamia furfuracea*) | Full sun | Low | Wind, heat, and salt tolerant |
| Coontie (*Zamia integrifolia*) | Partial shade | Mod | Slow grower |
| Hottentot's Head (*Stangeria eriopus*) | Partial shade | High | Not heat or salt tolerant |
| Karoo cycad (*Encephalartos lehmannii*) | Full sun | Mod | Heat, salt, and wind tolerant |
| King Sago palm (*Cycas revoluta*) | Full sun, partial shade | Low | Wind and salt tolerant |
| Macdonnell Range cycad (*Macrozamia macdonnellii*) | Full sun | Low | Heat and salt tolerant |
| Mexican Horncone (*Ceratozamia mexicana*) | Partial shade | Mod | Easy to grow |
| Queen Sago palm (*Cycas circinalis*) | Full sun, partial shade | Low | Wind and salt tolerant |
| Small-Spined cycad (*Dioon spinulosum*) | Full sun | Low | Wind tolerant |
| Wooly cycad (*Encephalartos villosus*) | Partial shade | High | Easy to grow |

Coontie (*Zamia integrifolia*)

(right): Mexican Weeping bamboo (*Otatea acuminata aztecorum*) in a bamboo basket.

(below): Lumpy Noodle bamboo (*Bambusa wamin*) in a glazed clay pot.

## BAMBOO

Outdoors, graceful, fine-leaved bamboo whispers whenever tropical breezes visit your lanai. Many bamboo prefer to be in indirect or full sun, and filtered sun is best for them in hot, dry conditions. Other bamboo varieties require some shade and cooler upland

temperatures. Bamboo needs excellent drainage, so you should lighten the potting mix with enough cinder or perlite. As for types of containers, porous terra-cotta pots are the happiest homes for bamboo. Bamboo does well with ample water, but roots left standing in water too long can rot. Remove excess runoff from the saucer or cachepot soon after watering, and let bamboo dry between waterings. Depending on the environment, bamboo in containers may need to be watered daily. Watering plants in early morning or late afternoon is best. Fertilize regularly with a slow-release fertilizer formulated for foliage plants.

Indoors, a bright skylight and good air circulation are absolutely essential. Bamboo quickly loses vigor when exposed to air conditioning. Overwatering is the most common mistake made when keeping bamboo indoors. You might need to water only once or twice a week in the cool season, and more often during warm weather.

Bamboo can outgrow its container within a year or less. You can either move the plant

Peter Berg of Quindembo Bamboo on the Big Island. The sizes given here are approximate, not maximum, for plants grown in the ground. Bamboo in containers have their growth restricted, and so you can expect the height of the plant and the diameter of the culms (woody stems) to be less than that of bamboo planted in the ground. You can also prune bamboo to keep it smaller. Note that the *Himalayacalamus* and *Drepanostachyum* bamboo listed don't do well in coastal areas and are best in cooler mauka (upland) areas.

(left): Closeup of Lumpy Noodle bamboo (*Bambusa wamin*). Cane looks similar to Buddha Belly *(Bambusa ventricosa),* but is a bit wider in diameter.

(below): Monastery bamboo (*Thyrsostachys siamensis*), planted here in ground next to a Balinese garden lamp, can also be grown in containers.

up to a pot at least two sizes bigger or root prune it to keep it in the same pot. Don't use an oversize pot, as you may be tempted to overwater—again, a big no-no. Choose a container with a mouth at least as wide or wider than the bottom so that it will be easier to remove the roots from the pot. If you root prune you should do it in early spring, before bamboo sends out new shoots. To root prune, use pruners or a saw to cut off one to three inches of the bottom roots and one to three inches around the sides of the root mass. Prune carefully according to the size of the plant; prune a smaller one less than you would a larger one. Repot with new potting mix. Keep it in shade for two weeks, and fertilize lightly one month after root pruning.

## Bamboo Varieties for Lanai and Patio

In Hawai'i, bamboos that grow in clumps are the clear choice over running types, which are invasive and extremely difficult to remove once established. The bamboo listed here were recommended by Susan Ruskin and

| COMMON NAME | BOTANICAL NAME | HEIGHT (FT) | NOTES |
|---|---|---|---|
| Malay Dwarf | *Bambusa glaucophylla* | 12-20 | Tolerates some wind |
| Timor Black | *Bambusa lako* | 40-50 | Shiny black canes |
| Chinese Hedge Bamboo | *Bambusa multiplex* 'Alphonse Karr' | 20-25 | Tolerates wind, salt |
| Silver Stripe Hedge Bamboo | *Bambusa multiplex* 'Silverstripe' | 15 | Tolerates heat, sun, wind |
| Giant Timber Bamboo | *Bambusa oldhamii* | 40-50 | Tolerates wind |
| ----- | *Bambusa rigida* | 20-30 | Upright like *textilis* |
| Weaver's Bamboo | *Bambusa textilis* | 40 | Tolerates heat, sun, wind |
| Striped Buddha's Belly | *Bambusa ventricosa* 'Kimmei' | 40 | Will "belly " in container |
| Lumpy Noodle | *Bambusa wamin* | 15 | Swollen "belly" internodes |
| Fargesia Borinda | *Borinda fungosa* | 20 | Longish leaves; from Himalaya |
| Costa Rican Weeping Bamboo | *Chusquea coronalis* | 12-20 | Feathery, Japanese maple-like |
| ----- | *Chusquea liebmannii* | 35 | Taller than *coronalis* |
| ----- | *Dendrocalamus minor* | 25-30 | Needs large container |
| Khasia Bamboo | *Drepanostachyum khasianum* | 12-20 | Cool mauka, partial shade |
| ----- | *Drepanostachyum sengteeanum* | 30 | Cool mauka, partial shade |
| ----- | *Gigantochloa* 'Sumatra' | 60 | Striped canes |
| Tibetan Princess | *Himalayacalamus asper* | 20 | Cool mauka, partial shade |
| ----- | *Himalayacalamus falconeri* | 20-30 | Cool mauka, partial shade |
| Candy Cane Bamboo | *Himalayacalamus falconeri* 'Damarapa' | 20-30 | Cool mauka, partial shade |
| Blue Bamboo | *Himalayacalamus hookerianus* | 25-35 | Cool mauka, partial shade |
| Mexican Weeping Bamboo | *Otatea acuminata aztecorum* | 15-20 | Tolerates salt spray |
| Mayan Silver Bamboo | *Otatea glauca* 'Mayan Silver' | 20-25 | Silvery blue powder on canes |
| Sacred Bali Bamboo | *Schizostachyum brachycladum* | 30-40 | Green striped yellow canes |
| Monastery Bamboo | *Thrysostachys siamensis* | 25-30 | Tolerates wind, sun, shade |

So many ti plants, so little space. There are hundreds of varieties to enchant everyone from casual gardeners to serious collectors.

## *Cordyline fruticosa*
## TI PLANTS, KĪ

Nearly every Hawaiian home has the large, shiny green ti, or lāʻī. Ti is a highly valued heritage plant in the Islands, brought to the Islands by early Hawaiians in their great double-hulled canoes. Ti plants have a multitude of uses that continue to be a part of modern Island life. From backyard grills to *haute cuisine* kitchens, green ti leaves are a favorite way to wrap foods and impart flavor when steaming, barbecuing, serving, and storing. A lei is sometimes presented in a ti leaf wrapper, or pūʻolo. Traditional Hawaiian medicinal uses include using leaves to bandage an injury or cool a feverish forehead. Ti is also used in religious ceremonies, lei making, and hula. In olden times the sweet, starchy root was steamed and eaten. After the introduction of metal pots, an alcoholic beverage called ʻōkolehao was brewed from ti roots.

After green ti arrived in the Islands, many new kinds of ti plants were introduced, much to the delight of today's avid ti plant collectors who know that there are literally hundreds of types. Ti plant aficionados hunt for the newest hybrids in shades of green, yellow, white, red, orange, pink, purple, brown, and nearly black. Leaves run the gamut from crinkled, curly or straight, ribbon-like or broad, rounded or pointed, long or short. Ti plants can be shrubby or look like a feather duster. The mini-leaved types known as kāhili have an appearance that is associated with the well-known symbol of Hawaiian royalty of the same name. Ancient chiefs were fanned with the tops of ti plants, and this might have evolved into the feather standards familiar to us today.

Ti can be kept in containers on the lanai with little care. Some types of ti plants grow faster than others, and some need protection from direct sun to maintain their brilliant colors. Dwarf and slow-growing types require less frequent repotting. Try a mixed planting of a ti plant and a low groundcover such as ʻaeʻae or dwarf mondo grass. Ti plants require ample water, and they look fabulous with a mulch of cinder that also helps retain moisture. Plants that are allowed to dry will have leaves turning yellow, with tips turning brown. Fertilize as you would for other plants grown for their foliage, for example using a 19-6-12 or 14-14-14 slow-release fertilizer. Refrain from foliar feeding, as this sometimes causes the leaves to burn. If a plant gets too tall, you can cut it to 6 inches and it will regrow and branch out.

'Vanuatu' ti plant with native 'ae'ae (*Bacopa monnieri*) planted at the base.

'Kaua'i Rose' ti plant

Many kinds of ti plants will root in 2 to 4 weeks from cuttings as small as a 1-inch log, in 1:1 perlite/vermiculite or in potting mix alone. A cutting placed in media vertically will grow a single plant. Three-quarters buried horizontally, the cutting will sprout with several plants. You can also root cuttings topped with leaves by placing them in a decorative vase with water, making a simple, graceful display.

## Popular Ti Plant Varieties for Containers

Slow-growing, dwarf, and medium height ti plants are excellent choices for patio and lanai. Ti plants that prefer shade may be grown indoors if there is adquate indirect sunlight. Here are just a few of the many gorgeous varieties suitable for containers.

| NAME | LEAF SIZE | LEAF COLOR | LIGHT | NOTES |
|---|---|---|---|---|
| Baby Doll | 6" x 1 ½" | Bright pink, maroon, green | Shade | Dwarf |
| Bob Alonzo | 14" x 6" | Orange-yellow, green, creamy pink | Shade | Medium height |
| Haole Girl | 12" x 4" | Pale green, broad white edges | Sun/shade | Medium height |
| Hawaiian Flag | 17 ½ " x 3" | Yellow with green/maroon stripes | Shade | Slow grower |
| Hilo Rainbow | 16" x 4" | Green, maroon, yellow, pink | Shade | Medium height |
| Iwao Shimizu | 5" x 2" | Green with orange edges | Shade | Dwarf |
| Kauaʻi Rose | 8" x 4" | Pink to rose, some green | Shade | Medium height |
| Kauaʻi Rosebud | 10" x 5" | Bright rose to burgundy | Sun/shade | Slow grower |
| Kiwi | 8 ½" x 2" | Olive green w/yellow, pink edge | Shade | Slow grower |
| Laʻī | 30" x 4 ½" | Glossy green | Sun/shade | Common green ti |
| Lau Kea | 10" long | Green, white | Sun/shade | Medium height |
| Lilinoe | 15" x 3" | Red | Sun/shade | Medium height |
| Lovely Hula Hands | 6" x 2" | Green, broad pale pink edge | Sun/shade | Medium height |
| Pele's Smoke | 21" x 4 ½" | Olive black, black streaks | Sun/shade | Medium height |
| Purple Prince | 8 ½" x 2 ¾" | Mature green with violet | Shade | Slow grower |
| Will I's Gold | 14" x 6" | Green w/yellow, gold, pink | Sun/shade | Medium height |

Desert Rose *(Adenium obesum)*

## MORE PLANTS FOR HAWAIʻI CONTAINER GARDENING

### *Adenium obesum*
### Desert Rose, Mock Azalea
**☠ Poisonous sap**

Desert plant with thick, succulent stems and bright pink flowers. Native to the Arabian Peninsula and tropical Africa. **Light:** Full sun or bright indirect sun. **Tolerates:** Heat, salt spray, wind. **Planting & Care:** Needs well-draining potting mix formulated for cactus, or mostly cinder mix. Needs light watering, regular slow-release fertilizer. **Uses:** Blooms year-round on a sun-drenched patio or lanai. Also grown as bonsai. Good for hot, dry, sunny leeward areas.

African Lily *(Agapanthus praecox)*

### *Agapanthus praecox*
### African Lily

Tropical lily that grows to about 2 feet high. Blooms April to September. Native to South Africa, sometimes erroneously referred to as Lily of the Nile even though it did not originate anywhere near there. **Light:** Full sun to partial sun. **Tolerates:** Heat, some salt spray. **Planting & Care:** Use well-draining potting mix. Thrives with regular slow-release fertilizer, regular watering. Easy to grow. Cut off dead flower stalks after flowering. **Uses:** Grow singly in a pot as an accent, or group several in a large container on patio or lanai. Flowering stalks are used in arrangements; tubular flowers can be strung into a single or double lei. **Varieties:** 'Albus' with white flowers; 'Mooreanus' with dark blue flowers; 'Nanus' and 'Peter Pan' are dwarf forms; 'Variegatus' has variegated foliage.

*Alocasia sanderiana*
**Kris Plant**

☠ **Poisonous parts. Like taro, leaves and stems contain calcium oxylate crystals that make those parts toxic.**

Striking, shiny, dark green foliage with contrasting silvery veins and margins. Grows to 2 feet high. Native to the Philippines. **Light:** Partial shade, bright indirect light. **Planting & Care:** Use rich, well-draining potting mix. Provide ample water and keep moist, feed lightly. **Uses:** In a pot on a shady lanai, protected from wind.

Kris Plant *(Alocasia sanderiana)*

*Aloe vera*
**Aloe, Pānini ʻawa ʻawa**

One of the easiest succulents to grow and useful, too. Grows 2 to 3 feet planted in ground, but stays smaller in a pot. **Light:** Full sun, partial shade. **Tolerates:** Wind, salt spray. **Planting & Care:** Plant in well-draining potting mix for succulents and cacti. Easy to grow, requires little fertilizer. Overwatering causes it to rot and die. Likes crowding, but you can remove keiki to plant in additional pots. Flowers in winter. **Uses:** A houseplant next to a sunny window, an accent in a pot outdoors on a lanai or doorstep. Place this medicinal in a convenient location by the kitchen. Peel the toothed leaves to use the gel-like sap to soothe sunburn and other minor skin irritations.

Aloe *(Aloe vera)*

## Anthurium, Spathe Flower

There are many anthurium hybrids with heart-shaped spathes in various shades of red, orange, pink, purple, white, and green. Wild species is native to Columbia and Equador. **Light:** Shade. **Planting & Care:** Requires excellent drainage; plant in a highly porous medium, such as cinders, redwood chips, or macadamia nut shells. Shredded hāpuʻu has long been a favorite medium, but supplies have been dwindling. The harvesting of hāpuʻu has had a negative impact on Hawaiʻi rain forests. Hāpuʻu grows slowly and more of these native tree ferns are being bulldozed to make way for development. Try using the other aforementioned media instead of hāpuʻu. Anthuriums need high humidity and regular watering. Use a balanced slow-release fertilizer or balanced liquid fertilizer applied as a drench to the roots. Good air circulation keeps the plant from developing fungal and bacterial diseases. Foliage can be pruned to as few as four healthy leaves without damaging the plant. Protect from wind and salt spray. **Uses:** Tropical floral display indoors or on a shady lanai or patio. Long-lasting as cut flowers. **Varieties:** Many excellent new varieties for pots are available, some with light fragrance.

Anthurium

## Bougainvillea, Pua Kepalō

**Thorns**

Many hybrids are available in a dazzling array of colors. Some plants have a vining habit, others are shrubby. Flowers are inconspicuous, but bracts are showy. Native to Brazil. **Light:** Full sun. **Planting and Care:** Grow in well-draining potting mix. Provide water regularly but do not overwater. Needs little fertilizer but blooms profusely with one high in phosphorus. Grows almost anywhere in Hawaiʻi and does especially well in dry, hot, sunny leeward areas. Prune to remove scraggly branches and to encourage more flowering. Flowers on new wood. **Uses:** Grow on a trellis as a screen; tie vines to the support. Dwarf-shrub types are best for pots. Can be pruned as a small tree or bonsai. Also good in hanging baskets. **Varieties:** 'California Gold'; 'Mary Palmer' bicolor with pink and white bracts; 'Miss Manila' with orange and purple bracts; 'Raspberry Ice' with variegated leaves and magenta bracts.

Bougainvillea

## Bromeliads

**☠ Some have sharp-toothed or sharp-pointed leaves**

The pineapple family is not native to Hawai'i, but it has a long economic history in the Islands. There are so many colorful varieties that enthusiasts seem to never run out of plants to add to their collections. Bromeliads are found wild in tropical America and western Africa, from deserts to high-elevation rain forests. **Light:** Ranges from full sun to shade, depending on the species. **Planting & Care:** Needs well-draining potting mix. Rainwater is ideal for bromies, since the chlorine in tap water can cause the leaves of some varieties to turn yellow. Keiki can be removed from the base and potted. **Uses:** Grow potted bromeliads on the lanai, in dish gardens, in planter boxes, and in mixed plantings. Many tillandsias are "air plants" that need practically no care at all except occasional misting in dry weather and a monthly dose of liquid fertilizer, also applied by misting. **Varieties:** Some popular bromeliads for containers are Blushing Bromeliad, *Neoregelia carolinae*; Pink Quill, *Tillandsia cyanea;* King of Bromeliads, *Vriesia hieroglyphica*; Imperial Vriesia, *Vriesia imperialis*; Silvery Vriesia, *Vriesia* aff. *regina*; Silver Vase, *Aechmea fasciata*.

Bromeliad *Guzmania lingulata* 'Variegata'

Dwarf Caladium 'Miss Muffett'

## Caladium, Kalo Kalakoa

**☠ Poisonous tubers (if eaten raw)**

Highly ornamental foliage in a multitude of color variations in red, pink, white, and green. Native to habitats from Costa Rica to Brazil. **Light:** Light shade, some can tolerate full sun if conditions are moist. **Planting & Care:** Plant in shallow containers about 7 inches high. Needs ample water, protection from wind and salt spray. Plants die back in winter to spring. Divide tubers while dormant. Easy to grow. **Uses:** Grow singly or grouped in combinations, in pots and planters outdoors on a shaded lanai. Also good for interiorscapes.

Zebra Plant, *Calathea zebrina* 'Humilior'

## Calathea

Calatheas are easy to grow in Hawai'i's year-round warm weather, making them popular foliage plants in the Islands. Native to the tropics of the New World. **Light:** Shade or partial shade. **Planting & Care:** All calatheas need ample moisture, rich potting mix, and shaded or partly shaded locations that are sheltered from the wind. **Uses:** All calatheas can be kept in containers outdoors on a shady lanai or indoors with filtered light.

Coffee (*Coffea arabica*)

## *Coffea arabica*
## Coffee

Coffee was introduced to the Hawaiian Islands in the early 1800s. The first coffee tree was planted in Mānoa, O'ahu. More trees were propagated in a small field there, and these trees were distributed to other areas of O'ahu and the neighbor Islands. The first large coffee plantation was established in Hanalei Valley in Kaua'i, but it collapsed due to coffee blight. Coffee was introduced to Kona in 1828; today, the Big Island accounts for most of the commercial coffee production. Hawai'i is the only state in the nation where coffee is grown commercially, and it is planted on all Islands as an agricultural crop. Native to tropical Africa. **Light:** Shade, bright indirect light. **Planting & Care:** Plant coffee in rich, well-draining potting mix. Keep moist, fertilize regularly. Plants must be 3 to 4 years old before they can develop fragrant white flowers and berries. Protect from wind. **Uses:** Coffee has deep green, glossy foliage that makes it an attractive small tree for the lanai or interiors.

### *Coleus x hybridus* (*Solenostemon scutellarioides*)
### Coleus, Spur Flower

Brightly colored foliage in shades of red, purple, brown, and nearly black. Native to East Africa. **Light:** Strong indirect sunlight, light shade. **Planting & Care:** Plant in rich, well-draining potting mix. Keep moist and provide a high nitrogen, slow-release fertilizer. Pinch off flower spikes to extend the life of the plant and to keep it bushy. Red-leaved plants are more sun-tolerant. Easy to grow. **Uses:** Hanging baskets, combination plantings. Can thrive outdoors or indoors with enough light. Roots easily from cuttings, so share some with a friend.

*Coleus x hybridus*

'Uahi-a-Pele', "Smoke of Pele" in an antique wooden tub

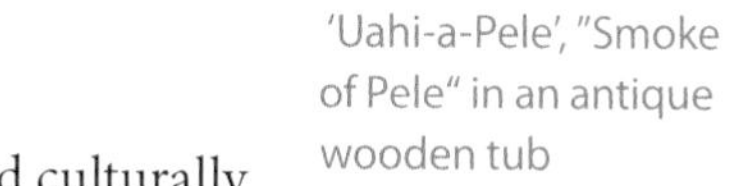

### *Colocasia esculenta*
### Taro, Kalo

Taro is the most historically and culturally significant food plant in Hawai'i. It might have originated in Southeast Asia; however it is found throughout Polynesia, where it continues to be an important dietary staple. **Light:** Full sun, light shade. **Planting & Care:** Grow taro as an edible or an ornamental. To accomodate the large edible corm, use a pot 12 to 16 inches in diameter, 8 to 10 inches deep. Plant huli (sets) or 'ohā (suckers) 6 to 10 inches deep in in rich, organic potting mix. Provide ample water, keep moist with a cover of mulch. Taro prefers high humidity, and to achieve this in dry areas UH extension recommends a double-potting method: Line the bottom of a larger pot with moist sphagnum moss, then place the planting pot inside it. Fill in the inner spaces between the two pots with more moist sphagnum moss. Use a balanced slow-release fertilizer when planting, and supplement with a balanced liquid fertilizer each week. If you want to harvest the leaves, wait until the plant is established. To harvest the corm, stop fertilizing after 6 months, and dig up at 8 to 10 months. Even if you don't harvest, divide the plant when leaves start getting smaller. **Uses:** In water gardens, in mixed plantings, or solitary in large pots. **Varieties:** Edible ornamentals include 'Uahi-a-Pele', 'Elepaio', 'Lehua Maoli Maui', 'Manini 'ōpelu', "Ele'ele naioea', 'Manini 'uli'uli', 'Piko lehua-āpi'i', "Ula'ula kūmū', "Ulu'ula poni', and 'Pue uta'. Some kinds of taro are grown only as ornamentals, and these usually have dark-violet coloration, including 'Euchlora', 'Fontenesii', 'Illustris', and 'Black Magic'.

'Elepaio' variegated taro

Croton 'Pele's Fire'

## *Codiaeum variegatum*
## Croton

Multihued leaves can be yellow, green, red, brown, almost purple, in a wide variety of forms, from broad to narrow to almost grass-like blades. Bright color and easy care make croton a perennial favorite in the Isles. **Light:** Partial shade to full sun. **Planting & Care:** Plant in potting mix that is somewhat acidic. Provide ample moisture, regular fertilizer. Foliage color is at its peak in bright sunlight, if plant is given enough water. However, croton is also somewhat drought tolerant. Prune to keep compact size, but be careful because sap permanently stains clothing. **Uses:** Can be planted individually in pots; does well in combination plantings. Combine different varieties for spectacular effects.

## Dracaena

Many dracaenas have lush foliage and can be grown under a range of light conditions. They thrive even with a little neglect. Native to Africa, Asia, northern Australia, Pacific Isles. **Light:** Partial shade. **Planting & Care:** Needs well-draining, rich potting mix. Keep moist, but make sure roots do not remain in water. Use balanced, slow-release fertilizer. Occasionally rinse the dust off leaves. Protect from wind, salt spray. Trimming off the top forces the plant to branch out. **Uses:** Usually several are planted in one pot to make it fuller. Use as a screen or a barrier on a shaded lanai. Also a popular indoor plant. **Varieties:** 'Janet Craig', 'Lindenii', 'Longii', 'Massangeana', 'Rothiana', 'Victoria', 'Compacta', 'Compacta Variegata', 'Warneckei'.

**Money Tree, *Dracaena marginata*,** is also popular for containers. The most common type of Money Tree has green leaves with red margins. 'Tricolor' has narrower leaves with pink, white, and green coloration. When this dracaena was first introduced in Hawai'i in the 1920s it was planted next to the Bishop Bank in Hilo, hence its common name. Some folks believe that if it grows over your house, you will have good fortune and be prosperous. **Light:** Full sun, partial shade. **Planting & Care:** Requires well-draining potting mix, regular fertilizer, and regular watering. **Tolerates:** Light salt spray, wind, dry conditions. Easy to grow. Cut stem tips to promote branching if desired. **Uses:** A low-maintenance potted plant on the lanai or indoors.

A close relative of the ti plant, dracaena can take many forms.

## *Euphorbia milii*
## Crown of Thorns

**☠ Very sharp thorns, poisonous sap**

Highly ornamental semisucculent with noticeably sharp thorns and bright red, pink, orange, or yellow flowers. Native to Madagascar. **Light:** Full sun. **Tolerates:** Salt spray, wind. **Planting & Care:** Plant in light, well-draining potting mix. Regular slow-release fertilizer. Tolerates some dryness but flowers more with regular water. Easy to grow. **Uses:** Grow in planters or pots; keep near a sunny window or on the lanai or patio. **Varieties:** Dwarf cultivars are best for small areas; those from Thailand have large flowers.

Crown of Thorns *(Euphorbia milii)*

## *Gardenia jasminoides*
## Gardenia, Kiele

Deeply fragrant white flowers contrast with dark green, glossy foliage, making gardenia a treasured plant in the Island landscape. Native to China, Japan, and Taiwan. **Light:** Full sun in cool areas, filtered sun in hot areas. **Planting & Care:** Grow in rich, well-draining, acidic (pH 5.0-6.0), organic potting mix. Use fish emulsion or a fertilizer made for acid-loving plants. Water regularly; keep moist but not soggy. In areas with low humidity, put the pot on a tray with clean pebbles partially filled with water. Needs cool nights (60-62°F) for flowering in late spring through early summer. Buds will drop if plant is exposed to low humidity and high heat. Will not flower in shade. **Uses:** Grow in tubs or pots outdoors on a sunny lanai or porch. Cut blossoms are lovely floating in a crystal bowl. Varieties: Excellent for small containers are 'Veitchii' and dwarf varieties 'White Gem' and 'Radicans'. 'August Beauty', 'Belmont', 'First Love', 'Mystery' are larger but suitable for large pots or tubs.

*Gardenia augusta* 'Radicans' is simply dazzling in a blue and white Chinese pot.

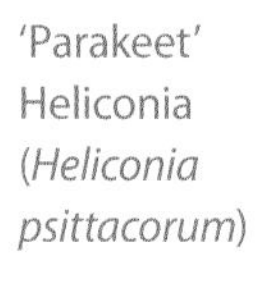

'Parakeet' Heliconia (*Heliconia psittacorum*)

## Heliconia

Relatives of the banana family, Heliconias have a tropical appearance yet none are native to Hawai'i. Most Heliconia need a fairly large space in the garden to grow, but some varieties of Parrot Heliconia (*Heliconia psittacorum*,) a native of South America, make fine container plants. **Light:** Full sun, partial shade. **Tolerates:** Wind, salt spray, lower humidity than other heliconias. **Planting & Care:** Needs well-draining, rich, acidic, organic potting mix. Provide ample water in hot, dry, leeward areas. Divide rhizomes and repot. **Uses:** Parrot Heliconia is actually better planted in containers than in the garden, since it can be invasive. Flowers are used in arrangements and lei making. **Varieties:** Dwarf 'Parakeet' is excellent for containers. Also recommended are 'Andromeda' and 'Kaleidoscope' (or 'Sassy'). Dwarf Jamaican Heliconia (*Heliconia stricta* 'Dwarf Jamaican') does well in containers. Dwarf Jamaican Heliconia grows only 2 feet tall and requires shade, moisture, and protection from wind.

## Hibiscus

Although most of them last only a day, the five-petaled blossoms are so beloved as symbols of the natural beauty of the Islands that they are frequently included in images of Hawai'i from advertising to fine art. There are several rare native Hawaiian hibiscus, even a few that have a soft fragrance. The state flower, Ma'o hau hele, is a native yellow hibiscus with a different species on nearly all of the Islands. Native hibiscus are popular in the garden and grow well with plenty of room to roam. Although native hibiscus is better planted in the ground, Common Red Hibiscus, sometimes called Chinese Hibiscus (*Hibiscus rosa-sinensis*), has dwarf and shrub-type hybrids suitable for containers. Hybrid flowers come in many colors and variations, and foliage can be variegated. **Light:** Full sun, light shade. **Tolerates:** Heat, salt. **Planting & Care:** Hibiscus needs well-draining potting mix. Regular fertilizer and regular watering produce blooms year-round. Some hibiscus, especially ones with red flowers, are susceptible to the erineum mite, which causes deformation of the foliage. Consult your local extension office for the latest information on controls. **Uses:** Grow dwarf varieties in pots on a sunny lanai or porch. Shrubby type can also be trained as a small tree.

Hibiscus hybrids

## *Impatiens hawkeri*
## New Guinea Impatiens

New Guinea Impatiens is larger and more sun tolerant than its shade-loving cousin, the common bedding impatiens or Busy-Lizzie (*Impatiens walleriana*). Like many annuals sold in Hawai'i, Busy-Lizzie grows as a perennial but gets leggy and leafless on the lower half within a year or two. It also tends to be invasive in higher elevation forests. New Guinea Impatiens is better suited for Hawai'i's climate and can be kept attractive longer. **Light:** Shade to filtered sun. **Planting & Care:** New Guinea Impatiens is easy to grow in regular potting mix. Provide ample water, regular slow-release fertilizer. Pinch tips to make the plant more compact. **Uses:** In pots and planters, alone or in mixed plantings. Place on the lanai or a front entryway for a welcoming burst of color.

New Guinea Impatiens 'Burgundy' (*Impatiens hawkeri* 'Burgundy')

## *Ipomoea batatas*
## Sweet Potato Vine, ʻUala

Fast-growing, trailing vine native to the American tropics. How did ʻuala get to Polynesia? Sweet potato existed in the Polynesian diet before the time of Columbus, prompting the theory that there was contact between Polynesia and the Americas before Columbus' time. **Light:** Full sun, partial shade. **Planting & Care:** Sweet potato can be grown as an edible and/or ornamental. Grow in regular, well-draining potting mix; provide ample water. If grown for foliage, use a balanced slow-release fertilizer. Use a fertilizer lower in nitrogen and higher in phosphorus if growing to harvest sweet potatoes. **Uses:** To grow it as an ornamental, plant it in hanging baskets or use as a trailing plant in combination plantings; grow in half barrels, raised beds, or tire planters if growing for the edible root. Young shoots and leaves used in Thai, Filipino, and Vietnamese dishes. **Varieties:** Ornamental types include 'Blackie' with dark purple, almost black leaves; 'Margarita' with heart-shaped, glowing chartreuse leaves; and 'Tricolor' with leaves of green, white, and tinge of pink.

'Blackie' and 'Margarita' sweet potato vines (*Ipomoea batatas*)

## Ixora

Flowers of this plant were offered to the Malabar deity Iswara, from which the name Ixora was derived. Many Ixora are native to Southeast Asia. **Light:** Full sun. **Planting & Care:** Plant in well-draining, acidic potting mix. Give ample water and keep moist. Can develop sooty mold due to mealybugs, scale, aphids; control with insecticidal soap or consult your local extension office. If leaves become yellow, it could be a sign of an iron deficiency. Use a fertilizer that contains micronutrients and is formulated for acid- loving plants. **Uses:** Flowers bloom profusely in clusters, adding vibrant color to a sunny patio, lanai, or doorstep. Compact habit makes Ixora a popular container plant. **Varieties:** Dwarf Thai forms are only 18 inches tall, perfect for small spaces. Flowers come in orange, pink, red, yellow, and white. 'Red King' is an old fashioned, large-headed variety.

Ixora

### *Jasminum sambac*
### Arabian Jasmine, Pīkake

The small, white, many-petaled blossoms have a scent that Princess Ka'iulani found so magnificent she named the plant pīkake after one of her favorite birds, the peacock. Also known as *sampagita*, the national flower of the Philippines. Cultivated for centuries in tropical Asia, uncertain origin. **Light:** Full sun for best blooming. Tolerates: Heat. **Planting & Care:** Plant in rich, well-draining potting mix with a pH of 5.5-7.0. Pīkake has a vining habit and must be pruned regularly to keep compact and encourage flowering. Fertilize after flowering. Flowers bloom in summer, releasing fragrance in the morning. Avoid watering leaves and flowers, or they might turn brown. **Uses:** Pīkake thrives in hot, dry areas on a sunny patio or lanai. Single-flowered types are preferred for lei making. Pīkake is also used to scent jasmine tea in China, and various plant parts are used medicinally throughout Asia.

Pīkake (*Jasminum sambac*)

*Leea guineensis* 'Burgundy'

### *Leea guineensis*
### *Leea*, West Indian Holly

This small tree from West Africa is easy to grow. **Light:** Full sun to shade. **Planting & Care:** Grow in rich, well-draining potting mix. Provide ample moisture, slow-release fertilizer. *Leea* have pearl glands from which sap oozes and hardens, forming harmless small beads on the foliage. Does not tolerate wind or salt spray. Red flowers appear in spring and summer, followed by red or black fruits. **Uses:** Excellent tree for interiorscapes; outdoors in pot at an entryway, as a screen on the lanai. **Varieties:** 'Rubra' is a red variety; 'Burgundy' has dark purple foliage.

Heavenly Bamboo (*Nandina domestica*)

### *Nandina domestica*
### Heavenly Bamboo, Sacred Bamboo

Not a true bamboo but a member of the barberry family, although it looks like its namesake with its cane-like stems. Emerging new leaves have a touch of pink and bronze. White flowers bloom in early spring to summer, followed by shiny red berries in the fall. Heavenly Bamboo is a translation of the Chinese name, *tian zhu*. Native to China and Japan. **Light:** Full sun, or partial shade in hot areas. **Tolerates:** Wind, dry areas if given ample water. **Planting & Care:** Needs regular well-draining potting mix and light applications of slow-release fertilizer. Does better at higher, cooler elevations. **Uses:** As a screen on the patio or lanai outdoors, massed in planters or planted singly in pots to accent Asian themes. Often planted to the left of the entrance of Japanese-style homes, as it is thought to ward off evil. Dwarf types also used for bonsai. **Varieties:** 'Atropurpurea Nana', 'Fire Power', 'Gulf Stream', 'Harbour Dwarf', 'Moon Bay', 'Compacta' ('Nana'), 'San Gabrial' ('Kurijusi', 'Orihime'), 'Alba'.

Ponytail Plant (*Nolina recurvata*) in a locally handmade pot by RYH Pottery.

### *Nolina recurvata*
### Ponytail Plant

As the name suggests, the young plant looks like a potato sticking up out of the pot with a tall-grass "hairdo." Native to Mexico. **Light:** Full sun or bright indirect light. **Tolerates:** Dry conditions, light salt spray. **Planting & Care:** Needs porous, well-draining potting mix. Do not overwater. Grows slowly, easy to maintain. **Uses:** Excellent as a houseplant in a spot near a sunny window, or outdoors with a collection of succulents and cacti in individual pots on a patio or lanai.

### *Ophiopogon japonicus*
### Mondo Grass, Dwarf Lilyturf

Grass-like ground cover native to Japan, China, and Korea. **Light:** Full sun to shade. **Tolerates:** Some salt spray, dry areas once established. **Planting & Care:** Grow in regular, well-draining potting mix. Provide ample water when establishing. Can tolerate some dryness, but prefers moist conditions. Use a slow-release fertilizer incorporated into the mix in the initial planting; thereafter, use liquid fertilizer. Grows slowly, easy to grow. **Uses:** At the base of a potted palm, bromeliad, or ti plant; in mixed plantings; or in a small individual pot. Blends well with Japanese-themed plantings such as Heavenly Bamboo and Yeddo Hawthorn. **Varieties:** There are several dwarf forms. Another type of dwarf mondo grass is Black Mondo Grass or 'Nigrescens', *Ophiopogon planiscapus.*

Dwarf mondo grass (*Ophiopogon japonicus*)

### *Pelargonium x hortorum*
### Zonal Geranium, Garden Geranium

Although it is commonly called geranium in Hawai'i, this bright, cheerful plant is actually *Pelargonium,* an easy-care perennial native to South Africa. **Light:** Full sun or bright indirect sun. **Tolerates:** Heat, dry areas. **Planting & Care:** Pelargoniums like being somewhat potbound, ideally in a clay pot with fast-draining potting mix. Allow to dry between waterings and don't overwater. A regular slow-release fertilizer is sufficient. Encourage continuous blooming by removing spent flowers. Can become leggy. Pinching tips results in a fuller plant. **Uses:** Mass in planters on a sunny lanai, line a stairway with vibrant color in clay pots. Place near a sunny kitchen window with a collection of culinary herbs. Match bright white flowers with clear reds and pinks. **Varieties:** Regular types can grow 3 to 4 feet tall in planters; dwarf types are best for small pots.

*Pelargonium,* often sold as zonal geranium, needs a sunny, dry location such as this windowsill.

Dwarf Singapore Plumeria (*Plumeria obtusa*)

## *Plumeria obtusa*
## Dwarf Singapore Plumeria

An elegant, petite version of an old-time favorite, native to the Bahamas. **Light:** Full sun. **Tolerates:** Heat, dry areas, some salt spray. **Planting & Care:** Plant in rich, well-draining potting mix. Drops leaves in winter, blooms spring through fall. **Uses:** Dwarf Singapore Plumeria is low growing and shrubby, an excellent plant for a sunny lanai or porch. Flowers of this plumeria are lightly scented and delicate. While the common plumeria (*Plumeria rubra*) loses its leaves during the year, Singapore plumeria is semievergreen and keeps most of its rounded, shiny leaves all year.

Portulaca (*Portulaca grandiflora*)

## *Portulaca grandiflora*
## Portulaca, Moss Rose

Succulent trailing plant with singular or double flowers in pink, red, white, or yellow. Native to South America. **Light:** Full sun. **Tolerates:** Heat. **Planting & Care:** Use regular potting mix. Portulaca is easy to grow but requires good drainage. Fertilize every six months. Cut back stems to stimulate new growth if necessary. **Uses:** In pots alone, in combinations as a trailing layer, in hanging baskets. **Varieties:** Most bloom mainly in the morning, but 'Afternoon Delight' and 'Sundance' bloom late into the day. There are several native portulaca, called ʻIhi in Hawaiian. *Portulaca molokiniensis* is a striking, rare, native plant that is sometimes available in nurseries. The leaves are very succulent, attractively arranged in rosettes. A leafless, upright stem bears clusters of stunning lemon-yellow blossoms. Plant in 1:1 potting mix to cinders or perlite to ensure good drainage. Incorporate a slow-release fertilizer into the potting mix before planting.

### *Rhaphiolepis umbellata*
### Yeddo Hawthorn, Kokutan

Slow-growing shrub with leathery dark green leaves and small, lightly fragrant white or pink flowers. Native to Japan and Korea. **Light:** Full sun, partial shade. **Tolerates:** Salt, heat, dry areas. **Planting & Care:** Plant in well-draining potting mix with a pH of 6.0-6.5. Needs regular water, regular fertilizing. Takes pruning well. **Uses:** A handsome potted plant for a sunny patio or lanai. Used in bonsai and Asian-themed gardens.

Yeddo Hawthorn (*Rhaphiolepis umbellata*)

Bird of Paradise (*Strelitzia reginae*), the quintessential tropical flower

### *Strelitzia reginae*
### Bird of Paradise

Distinctive blue and orange flowers of the Bird of Paradise have long been a popular exotic in tropical gardens. Native to coastal Southern Africa. **Light:** Full sun. **Tolerates:** Some salt spray. **Planting & Care:** Needs rich, well-draining potting mix with a pH of 5.5–6.5. Provide ample water. Allow plant to clump and get crowded in the container. Bird of Paradise does not take well to being divided and repotted and is slow to recover. Use a balanced slow-release fertilizer. **Uses:** Excellent in containers near a pool, in a sunny corner of a deck, or lanai. Cut flowers last two weeks or more and are popular in arrangements and floral decorations for special events.

Purple Heart
(Tradescantia pallida
'Purpurea')

### *Tradescantia pallida* 'Purpurea'
### Purple Heart, Purple Queen

Deep purple stems and leaves are an unusual contrast to its small pink flowers. Spreading habit, easy to grow. Native to Mexico. **Light:** Full sun, light shade. **Tolerates:** Heat. **Planting & Care:** Plant in a light, well-draining potting mix. Provide regular watering, regular fertilizer. **Uses:** Allow to spill over the sides of hanging baskets and pots. Can be used as part of a mixed planting in a large container.

# 10 Resources for Container Gardening

University of Hawai'i at Mānoa, College of Tropical Agriculture and Human Resources (UH CTAHR) Cooperative Extension Service provides research-based information to the gardening public. If you need help troubleshooting a specific problem, call your local office and get free information from an Extension agent or a Master Gardener volunteer. There are fees for laboratory testing and diagnostics of soils, water quality, and plant pests.

## UH CTAHR COOPERATIVE EXTENSION OFFICES

### Hawai'i

UH CTAHR
Cooperative Extension Service
67-5189 Kamāmalu Road
Kamuela, HI 96743
(808) 887-6183

UH CTAHR
Cooperative Extension Service
875 Komohana Street
Hilo, HI 96720
(808) 981-5199

UH CTAHR
Cooperative Extension Service
79-7381 Māmalahoa Highway
Kealakekua, HI 96750
(808) 322-4892

## Kaua'i

UH CTAHR
Cooperative Extension Service
State Office Building
3060 'Eiwa Street, Room 210
Līhu'e, HI 96766
(808) 274-3471

## Maui County

UH CTAHR
Cooperative Extension Service
310 Ka'ahumanu Avenue, Bldg. 214
Kahului, HI 96732
(808) 244-3242

## Moloka'i

UH CTAHR
Cooperative Extension Service
P.O. Box 394
Ho'olehua, HI 96729
(808) 567-6929

## O'ahu

UH CTAHR
Cooperative Extension Service
1955 East-West Road, Ag Sci III Room 217
Honolulu, HI 96822
(808) 956-7138

UH CTAHR
Cooperative Extension Service
45-260 Waikalua Road, Ste. 101
Kāne'ohe, HI 96744
(808) 247-0421

CTAHR
Cooperative Extension Service
Urban Garden Center
955 Kamehameha Highway
Pearl City, HI 96782
(808) 453-6050

UH CTAHR
Cooperative Extension Service
910 California Avenue
Wahiawā, HI 96786
(808) 622-4185

## SUPPLIERS

Experienced store personnel understand the growing conditions of your area and can provide good advice. Big-box chain stores are known for carrying large quantities of basic garden supplies. However, it is a good idea to support locally owned garden retailers who have an inventory specifically geared to your area. Some even have unusual plants from small growers. Small businesses usually will take special orders.

Included here are small retail businesses that have good selections of plants suitable for container growing. Many also sell containers, potting mix, fertilizers, garden sculpture, and pottery.

## LOCAL RETAILERS

### Hawai'i

Garden Exchange
300 Keawe Street
Hilo, HI 96720
(808) 961-2875
Plants, containers, supplies, garden accents & statuary.

Kainaliu Gardens
79-7372 Māmalahoa Highway
Kealakekua, HI 96750
(808) 322-3006
Plants, small to large pottery, supplies, garden accents & statuary.

Mohala Pua Garden Center
P.O. Box 236
Honoka'a, HI 96727
(808) 775-9800
Plants, containers, supplies, garden accents & statuary.

Paradise Plants
40 Wiwo'ole Street
Hilo, HI 96720
(808) 935-4043
Plants, containers, supplies, Southeast Asian imports & statuary.

Rozett's Nursery
HCR 1 Box 5081
Kea'au, HI 96749
(808) 982-5422
Plants, potting mix, supplies.

Sunrise Nursery
73-4939 Kamanu Street
Kailua-Kona, HI 96740
(808) 329-7593
Plants, containers, supplies, Southeast Asian garden accents & statuary.

### Kaua'i

Garden Ponds Nursery
5-2719A Kūhiō Highway
Kīlauea, HI 96754
(808) 828-6400
Water gardening containers and supplies, pottery, plants, sacred art & statuary.

Kaua'i Nursery and Landscaping
3-1550 Kaumuali'i Highway
Līhu'e, HI 96766
(808) 245-7747
Neighbor Islands call toll free
1 (888) 345-7747
www.kauainursery.com
Plants, imported pottery, potting mix, supplies, garden accents & statuary.

## Maui

Ki Hana Nursery
1746A S. Kīhei Road
Kīhei, HI 96753
(808) 879-1165
Plants, supplies, potting mix, small to large pottery from Southeast Asia, statuary.

Kula True Value Hardware & Nursery
3100 Lower Kula Road
Kula, HI 96790
(808) 876-0734
Plants, potting mix, supplies, wide variety of containers, large pottery, fountains, garden accents & statuary.

## O'ahu

Glenn's Flowers and Plants
41-513 Flamingo Street
Waimānalo, HI 96795
(808) 259-9625
Plants, nursery-blended potting mix, locally handmade pottery.

Ko'olau Farmers, Kailua
1127 Kailua Road
Kailua, HI 96734
(808) 263-4414
Plants, containers, supplies, potting mix, garden accents.

Ko'olau Farmers, Kāne'ohe
45-580 Kamehameha Highway
Kāne'ohe, HI 96744
(808) 247-3911
Plants, containers, supplies, potting mix, garden accents.

Ko'olau Farmers, Honolulu
1199 Dillingham Boulevard, Unit C109
Honolulu, HI 96817
(808) 843-0436
Plants, containers, supplies, potting mix, garden accents.

Star Garden Supply, Moili'ili
2470 S. King Street
Honolulu, HI 96826
(808) 564-7688
Plants, containers, supplies, potting mix.

Tropical Garden Accents
41-659A Waikupanaha Street
Waimanalo, HI 96795
(808) 259-9851
www.tgaccents.com
Over 3 acres of pottery, large urns for water gardens, plants, garden accents, sacred art and statuary from Southeast Asia, India, China.

Wally's Garden Center
1935 S. Beretania Street
Honolulu, HI 96826
(808) 947-2663
Plants, potting mix, plastic containers.

## GARDEN SPECIALTIES

### Cast Stone

Big Rock Manufacturing Inc.
1050 Kikowaena Place
Honolulu, HI 96819
On O'ahu call (808) 834-7625
Neighbor Islands call toll free
1(866) 344-ROCK (7625)
www.bigrockhawaii.com
Lightweight cast stone pots, benches, Asian-style statuary, fountains, stone wall veneers.

Natural Hawaiian Island Stone
669 Āhua Street
Honolulu, HI 96819
(808) 488-9188
www.rockstogo.com
Asian and Hawaiian-themed stone garden accents, statuary.

### Garden Art

Volcano Garden Arts
Ira Ono, founder/director
19-3834 Old Volcano Road
Volcano, HI 96785
(808) 985-8979
www.volcanogardenarts.com
Art for the garden.

Sacred Stone Garden Art
Deborah Bridges, artist
P.O. Box 1934
Nevada City, CA 95959
(530) 274-7889
www.sacredstone.net
Garden sculpture from cast stone and lightweight aggregates.

### Custom Pottery

Tropical Clay
41-829 Kaka'ina Street
Waimānalo, HI 96795
(808) 259-8600
www.tropicalclay.com
Locally handcrafted custom pottery up to 30" diameter.

### Lava Pots

Patti Datloff, artist, (808) 982-9838
Karen Hagen, artist, (808) 982-5150
HCR 1 Box 5280
Kea'au, HI 96749
gdatloff@juno.com/Karenhagen@aol.com
Lava-inspired pots of concrete.

Mark Kimball, artist
Kailua-Kona, HI
(808) 938-5666
lavapots@hawaii.rr.com
Composite lava pots up to 6 feet in diameter for water gardens, cachepots.

## Native Hawaiian Plants

Hui Ku Maoli Ola Native Hawaiian Plant Specialists
Rick Barboza & Matt Schirman
Kāneʻohe, HI
(808) 295-7777
nativehawaiianplants@gmail.com

## Non-Invasive Bamboo

Quindembo Bamboo
Susan Ruskin & Peter Berg
Kawaihae, HI
(808) 885-4968
www.bamboonursery.com
Ships within the state of Hawaiʻi.

## Ti Plants

Special Ti Nursery
Fred Stone & Debbie Ward
Kurtistown, HI 96760
(808) 966-7361
alohati450@aol.com
Over 400 varieties of ti plants.

Ti's Unlimited
David Yearian
Waimānalo, HI
(808) 259-6322

## Worm Composting

Hawaiʻi Rainbow Worms
Piper Selden, owner
905 Hoʻolauleʻa Street
Hilo, HI 96720
(808) 937-2233
www.hawaiirainbowworms.com
Hawaiian worms and worm bins, education and consultation.
Ships within the state of Hawaiʻi.

Waikiki Worm Co.
Mindy Jaffe, owner
234 ʻŌhua Avenue #118
Honolulu HI 96815
(808) 382-0432
www.waikikiworm.com
Hawaiian worms and worm bins, education and consultation.

# Bibliography

Abbott, Isabella Aiona. *Lāʻau Hawaiʻi: Traditional Hawaiian Uses of Plants.* Honolulu: Bishop Museum Press, 1992.

Bezona, Norman C., and Fred D. Rauch. *Palms in Hawaiian Gardens.* University of Hawaiʻi College of Tropical Agriculture and Human Resources, Research Extension Series 118, May 1990.

Bornhorst, Heidi L. *Growing Native Hawaiian Plants.* Honolulu: Bess Press, 2005.

Brenzel, Kathleen Norris, ed. *Western Garden Book.* Menlo Park, CA: Sunset Publishing Corporation, 2001.

Criley, Richard. *Enhancing Your Lanai, Balcony, or Patio with Container Plants.* University of Hawaiʻi Cooperative Extension Service, HG-43, August 2002.

Cusack, Victor. *Bamboo World*. Australia: Kangaroo Press, 1999.

Dawson, Helen. "Planters Cast in Stone." *Kitchen Gardener*, no. 4; 54-57. Taunton Press.

Department of Forestry and Wildlife, Department of Land and Natural Resources, state of Hawai'i. "Hawai'i's Most Invasive Horticultural Plants: An Introduction." Web page accessed on October 24, 2006. http://www.state.hi.us./dlnr/dofaw/hortweeds/

Ebesu, Richard. *Home Garden Tomato*. University of Hawai'i Cooperative Extension Service, HGV-5, May 2004.

Ebesu, Richard. *Home Garden Oriental Leafy Greens*. University of Hawai'i Cooperative Extension Service, HGV-10, May 2004.

Ebesu, Richard. *Home Garden Beans*. University of Hawai'i Cooperative Extension Service, HGV-8, May 2004.

Gillman, Jeff. *The Truth About Garden Remedies: What Works, What Doesn't, and Why*. Portland: Timber Press, 2006.

Hensley, David, and Jay Deputy. *Nandina (Heavenly Bamboo)*. University of Hawai'i Cooperative Extension Service, OF-26, April 2000.

Hensley, David, and Julie Yogi. *Substitutions for Peat in Hawai'i Nursery Production*. University of Hawai'i Cooperative Extension Service, HRN-11, November 1997.

Hepperly, Paul, Francis Zee, Russell Kai, Claire Arakawa, Mark Meisner, Bernard Kratky, Kert Hamamoto, and Dwight Sato. *Producing Bacterial Wilt-Free Ginger in Greenhouse Culture*. University of Hawai'i Cooperative Extension Service, SCM-8, June 2004.

Hodge, Peggy Hickock. *Gardening in Hawai'i*. Honolulu: Mutual Publishing, 1996.

Kobayashi, Kent, John Griffis, Andrew Kawabata, and Glenn Sako. *Hawaiian Ti*. University of Hawai'i Cooperative Extension Service, OF-33, March 2007.

Kobayashi, Kent, and Andrew J. Kaufman. *Common Gardenia*. University of Hawai'i Cooperative Extension Service, OF-32, May 2006.

Kratky, B.A. *A Simple Hydroponic Growing Kit for Short-Term Vegetables*. University of Hawai'i Cooperative Extension Service, HG-42, June 2002.

Kuepper, George, and Kevin Everett. *Horticulture Technical Note: Potting Mixes for Certified Organic Production*. Appropriate Technology Transfer for Rural Areas, National Center for Appropriate Technology, September 2004.

Lilleeng-Rosenberger, Kerin E. *Growing Hawai'i's Native Plants*. Honolulu: Mutual Publishing, 2005.

McCall, Wade W. *Soil Management for House Plants*. University of Hawai'i Cooperative Extension Service, General Home Garden Series No. 23, June 1980.

McCall, Wade W. *Basic Characteristics of Media for Container Grown Plants*. University of Hawai'i Cooperative Extension Service, General Home Garden Series No. 10, June 1980 reprint.

McCall, Wade W., Kenneth Y. Takeda, and Stephen K. Fukuda. *Container Grown Gardens*. University of Hawai'i Cooperative Extension Service, General Home Garden Series No. 32, July 1982.

Rauch, Fred D., and Paul R. Weissich. *Plants for Tropical Landscapes: A Gardener's Guide*. Honolulu: University of Hawai'i Press, 2000.

Pukui, Mary Kawena. *Ōlelo No'eau: Hawaiian Proverbs and Poetical Sayings*. Honolulu: Bishop Museum Press, 1983.

Roth, Sally, and Pamela K. Peirce. *Ortho's All About Container Gardening.* Des Moines, Iowa: Meredith Publishing, 2001.

Sakuoka, Richard, Randall T. Hamasaki, and Robin Shimabuku. *Lettuce for the Home Garden.* University of Hawai'i Cooperative Extension Service, HGV-2, April 2000. (Revised from earlier publication.)

Staples, George, and Michael Kristiansen. *Ethnic Culinary Herbs: A Guide to Identification and Cultivation in Hawai'i.* Honolulu: University of Hawai'i Press, 1999.

Staples, George W., and Derral R. Herbst. *A Tropical Garden Flora.* Honolulu: Bishop Museum Press, 2005.

Selden, Piper, Michael DuPonte, Brent Sipes, and Kelly Dinges. *Composting Worms for Hawai'i.* University of Hawai'i Cooperative Extension Service, HG-46, August 2005.

Selden, Piper, Michael DuPonte, Brent Sipes, and Kelly Dinges. *Small Scale Vermicomposting.* University of Hawai'i Cooperative Extension Service, HG-45, August 2005.

Takeda, Kenneth Y., and Richard T. Sakuoka. *Summer Squash.* University of Hawai'i Cooperative Extension Service, Home Garden Vegetable No. 15, January 1997.

Tanaka, Jack, Yukio Nakagawa, and Richard Sakuoka. *Bell Pepper.* University of Hawai'i Cooperative Extension Service, Home Garden Vegetable No. 3, January 1997.

Tanaka, Jack, and Richard T. Sakuoka. *Eggplant.* University of Hawai'i Cooperative Extension Service, Home Garden Vegetable Series No. 13, March 1978.

UH CTAHR. *Taro: Mauka to Makai.* Honolulu: College of Tropical Agriculture and Human Resources, University of Hawai'i at Manoa, 1997.

Valier, Kathy. *Ferns of Hawai'i.* Honolulu: University of Hawai'i Press, 1995.

Webster, Vicki. *Container Gardening.* Menlo Park, CA: Sunset Publishing, 2004.

# Index